Leading Issues in e-Learning Research

For researchers, teachers and students

Edited by

Mélanie Ciussi and Erik Gebers Freitas

Leading Issues in e-Learning Research
Volume One
Copyright © 2012 The authors

First published June 2012

Disclaimer: While every effort has been made by the editor, authors and the publishers to ensure that all the material in this book is accurate and correct at the time of going to press, any error made by readers as a result of any of the material, formulae or other information in this book is the sole responsibility of the reader. Readers should be aware that the URLs quoted in the book may change or be damaged by malware between the time of publishing and accessing by readers.

Note to readers.
Some papers have been written by authors who use the American form of spelling and some use the British. These two different approaches have been left unchanged.

ISBN: 978-1-906638-91-7 (print)
         978-1-908272-54-6 (e-Pub)

Printed by Good News Digital Books

Published by: Academic Publishing International Limited, Reading, RG4 9AY, United Kingdom, info@academic-publishing.org

Available from www.academic-bookshop.com

Contents

List of Contributing Authors

Monika Andergassen, *Leeds Metropolitan University, Leeds, UK*

Silvie Barma, *Laval University, Canada*

Reinhold Behringer, *Leeds Metropolitan University, Leeds, UK*

S Daniel, *Laval University, Canada*

Peter Duffy, *The Hong Kong Polytechnic University, Hong Kong*

Andrea Gorra, *Leeds Metropolitan University, Leeds, UK*

Sue Greener, *University of Brighton, UK*

Richard Hall, *De Montfort University, UK*

Rob Harrap, *Queen's University, Canada*

Ling-yi Huang, *National Chengchi University, Taipei, Taiwan*

Geraldine Jones, *University of Bath, UK*

David Moore, *Leeds Metropolitan University, Leeds, UK*

Pam Moule, *Faculty of Health and Social Care, University of the West of England, UK*

Michael Power, *Laval University, Canada*

Noeline Wright, *The University of Waikato, Hamilton New Zealand*

An Introduction to Leading Issues in e-Learning

E-learning is now fully part of our learning environment and no longer an add-on to traditional pedagogies. It is integrated in the way we live, work and teach and has been so since mid-2000 as Web 2.0 – the ReadWrite web (O'Reilly, 2005) – definitively displaced Web 1.0 in our daily affairs. Web 2.0 offers multiple advantages. One is due to its technology, which allows communication beyond physical frontiers, space and time. Another relates to its connectivity: it connects people and offers multiple ways to interact, including social networks, e-mail, blogs, wikis... And simple web services such as tags, comments, posts, feeds and votes open up yet other windows for interaction and sharing. And this changes everything.

Web 2.0 and social media introduce *Education* to a new paradigm that is founded on the notion of user-centric design. We are shifting from "traditional" e-learning modalities (lectures, notes, slide presentations, websites, on line quizzes) to a user-centric experience that involves collaborative and co-created learning products (wikis are the perfect example). In line with "communal constructivism" (Holmes, 2010), this e-learning evolution (not revolution) stresses changes in the fundamentals of teaching. The pressure for change comes from two angles: first, Web 2.0 tools offer additional interactivity and potentially more collaboration between peers, students and teachers; secondly, the Generation Y *Millennials* – the "Nintendo and Net Generation" (Tapscott, 1997; Oblinger, 2003) – prefer "on demand" access to media, are in constant communication with friends, visit their social network at least once a day (for 60% of them), and expect "twitch speed games" (Prensky, 2009) ... instant response and feedback. They also create their own content on the Internet – 57% of online teens according to Lenhard and Madden (2005) – and 20% post videos of themselves (http://blog.carbidemedia.com/post/19886836168/marketing-infographic-who-are-the-millennials).

Thus, pedagogy must evolve to integrate these new tools, develop new course scenarios and learning spaces. Web 2.0 points to inevitable challenges for the future of e-learning in terms of course content and design, assessment systems, student participation and informal/formal/non-formal learning spaces. Renée-Marie Fountain, a professor at Laval, uses wikis intensively in all her classes. In *Wiki Pedagogy*, she argues, *"...The collective tensions created by wikis — for those who dare to risk living them — may radically alter pedagogical praxis. Wikis' collective, open structure redistributes the traditional (i.e. academic) knowledge-power nexus along non-authoritative lines"* (Fountain, quoted by Audet p. 26). Teachers must partly abandon control over the transfer of knowledge as students build their own transfer systems, either individually or collectively.

A similar issue arises from mobile learning: with handheld devices such as tablets or smart phones, *"...the learning experience can take place in a variety of outdoor and indoor settings"* (Rogers et al., 2005, p. 56). Learning may thus be delivered "just in time" or "on the move". Teachers must confront the overlap between formal and informal learning (Sharples, 2006; Hodkinson and Colley, 2003), which emphasizes the dichotomy between teacher control of course content and evaluation, versus student control of devices and their learning (Ciussi, et al., 2009). As Kukulska-Hulme (2009, pg. 164) so aptly remarks, *"...what makes mobile technology so intriguing is that it has an affinity with movement between indoors and outdoors, across formal and informal settings, allowing learners to lead at least some of the way"*.

From a global perspective education systems must now embrace physical and virtual worlds, formal and informal settings, and personal and academic environments. New integrated curricula must be designed beyond the experimental stage. These are the premises of Education 3.0. If Education 2.0 is focused on use of Web 2.0 tools (Lemery, 2007), Education 3.0 encompasses all dimensions integrated in new course curriculum designs. This is more than shifting frontiers between online and face-to-face, or formal and informal learning; the frontiers as we commonly know them today simply disappear. The attributes of Education 3.0 as we view matters are presented in Table 1.

Table 1: Attributes of Education 3.0 (adapted from Ciussi and Despres, 2010, p.27)

	Traditional	1.0	2.0	3.0
1. Driver of the educational process	Professor-system			Student-team
2. Impetus to learn	Prof-Institution			Problem-situation
3. Type of learning	Reception-based (passive)			Inquiry-based (active)
4. Evaluation of progress	Grades / scholastic			Results / competencies
5. Curriculum organization	Disciplinary			Situation-based
6. Knowledge organization	Fragmented			Systemic
7. Real-world application	Later			Today
8. "Reality" is ...	Out there, one day			In here and now
9. Time is ...	Semester-based			Situation-based
10. Basis for successful curriculum	Course sequence & teaching			Situation design & coaching
11. Involvement of companies	In sequence, after courses			In the situation, real-time
12. Assessment	Summative and formative			Continuous feedback, self evaluation and peer assessment
13. Learning environment	Classrooms			Mobile, outside schools, Adaptable
14. Space	Unidimentional			Multidimensional/Interconnected

Education 3.0 can be implemented at an organizational level only with understanding and buy-in on the part of faculty and administration. The faculty culture must support online and innovative pedagogies, as evidenced in global teaching and learning strategies, and this often requires a teacher development program.

If Web 2.0 offers new ways to innovate from a pedagogical and organizational perspective, its applications are catalysts for a reflection on the future of education and in particular, distance learning. It is this latter horizon that we address in this book, specific to the context of higher education.

The spirit of this collection is to present the building blocks of Education 3.0. Each chapter proposes a specific view on distance learning using Web 2.0 applications, and the selection favors works that are innovative and complementary. The collection is also both empirical and practical: we have consciously chosen works that advance best practice resulting from experimentation.

The first article focuses on learning communities of practices and ad-dresses two issues: encouraging members to participate, share and learn; and secondly, supporting the acquisition of professional practice beyond academic topics. The second article focuses on the notion of a Personal Learning Environment (PLE) which highlights the tension between con-trolled or self-directed learning. Hall proposes a fused model of learning encompassing the two dimensions. The third, fourth and fifth chapters present experimentations with Web 2.0 tools in formal learning contexts. Both asynchronous tools (wikis, YouTube, blogs, twitter) and synchronous tools (Livechat) are examined. The sixth chapter differs from the others as it investigates spontaneous learning in an informal context, outside the traditional course settings. The seventh article is dedicated to innovative assessment methods with Web 2.0 tools (peer assessment), whereas the last two articles offer an innovative perspective on pedagogies based on *Mobile Gaming* – a combination of mobile learning and serious gaming. Thus, this collection offers a panorama of the main impacts of Web 2.0 in Education. They concern user-centric content, assessment systems, partic-ipation and interaction, mobile learning spaces and professorial control.

These works are derived from the latest research articles published in the *Electronic Journal of e-Learning* and refereed proceedings from the *Euro-pean Conferences on E-learning and Game-Based Learning*.

References

Audet, L. (2010). Wikis, blogues et Web 2.0 : Opportunités et impacts pour la formation à distance. Montréal, Canada : Réseau d'enseignement francophone à distance du Canada (REFAD).
http://refad.ca/nouveau/Wikis_blogues_et_Web_2_0.html

Ciussi, M., Rosner, G., & Augier, M. (2009). Engaging Students with Mobile Technologies to Support Their Formal and Informal Learning. *International Journal of Mobile and Blended Learning (IJMBL)*, 1(4), 84-98.

Ciussi, M. and Despres, C. (2010). INSPIRE: SKEMA Innovative Curriculum. A working group report, SKEMA Business School, Sophia Antipolis, France.

Hodkinson, P. and Colley, H. (2003). "The Interrelationships between In-formal and Formal Learning". Journal of Workplace Learning, 15(7-8), pp. 313 –318.

Holmes, B., Tangney, B., Fitzgibbon, N, A., Savage, T, & Mehan, S. (2001). *Communal Constructivism: Students constructing learning for as well as with others.* Centre for Research in IT in Education Trinity College Dublin, Ireland. https://www.cs.tcd.ie/publications/tech-reports/reports.01/TCD-CS-2001-04.pdf

Kukulska-Hulme, A. (2009). "Will mobile learning change language learning?" *ReCALL,* 21(2), pp 157–165. 2009, Cambridge University Press.

O'Reilly, T. (2005). "What Is Web 2.0? Design Patterns and Business Models for the Next Generation of Software. Web 2.0 Conference, O'Reilly Media. <http://www.oreillynet.com/pub/a/oreilly/tim/news/2005/09/30/what-is-web-20.html>

Sharples, M. (2006). "How can we address the conflicts between personal informal learning and traditional classroom education? *"Big Issues in Mobile Learning."* Report of a workshop by the *Kaleidoscope Network of Excellence in Mobile Learning* initiative, University of Nottingham. Retrieved online at: http://telearn.noe-kaleidoscope.org/warehouse/Sharples-2006.pdf

Prensky, M. (2001). *Digital game based Learning*. McGraw-Hill, New York, 442 pp

Tapscott, D. (1997). *Growing up Digital: the Rise of the Net Generation*, McGraw-Hill, New York

Oblinger D., (2003) Boomers, Gen-Xers, and Millennials : Understanding the "New" Students , EDUCAUSE Review, vol 38 n°4.

Rogers, Y., Price, C., Randell, S., Stanton, D., Weal, M. and Fitzpatrick, G. (2005). "Ubi-learning integrates indoor and outdoor experiences." Communications of the ACM - special issue: Interaction design and children, 48, pp. 55–59.

Leading Issues in e-Learning Research

Developing the Communities of Practice, Framework for Online Learning

Pam Moule
Faculty of Health and Social Care, University of the West of England, UK

Editorial Commentary

This paper presents a Communities of Practice (CoP) framework for online learning in higher education. CoPs address two important issues in e-learning: first, they support member participation, sharing and learning beyond simple content delivery; secondly, they encourage the development of professional practice beyond the scholastic aspects of a topic. Learning in CoPs is "situated" in professional practice: it is *knowing to be in practice* rather than *knowing about practice* (Brown and Duguid, 2002) and thus a more authentic learning environment is developed.

Moule explores social and situated learning theories in this chapter, reporting findings from a course entitled "Interprofessional Module" (IP3) that was designed as a CoP for health care students. Developments in this course laboratory drew on Wenger's three essential components for an effective community: mutual engagement, joint enterprise and shared repertoire.

The originality in IP3 lies in the augmented framework it deployed based on Wengerian foundations, and stemming from this Moule highlights a number of best practices for CoPs as online learning frameworks. To support *mutual engagement*, participants must be able to engage in dialogue, and thus master virtual communication tools such as discussions boards and virtual classrooms. The negotiation of meaning and decision-making is more effective in synchronous discussion. To establish *joint enterprise* the development of trust is essential, and course design should require students to

1

explore each other's stories and values. To develop *shared reper-toire*, the duration of a course module is important because a CoP lacks the richness of face-to-face interaction - gestures, voice and manifest routines. This education design around a CoP was not un-iformly positive, however, with some individuals failing to engage in community endeavor and preferring to work autonomously.

Abstract: Doctoral research considered whether healthcare students were able to develop characteristics of Communities of Practice when engaged in an interpro-fessional online module. Using a case study approach the research included two phases. Within phase one a questionnaire was administered to the group of 109 healthcare students. These were analysed to gain information on which to base sampling for the subsequent phase. Phase two employed three strands of data collection; five students completed an online diary, the online interaction of seven students was captured on a discussion board and three students were interviewed. Data were analysed using a form of pattern matching. The results suggested stu-dents were able to develop the essential elements of Communities of Practice. This was not uniformly seen however, and particular issues emerged for the online community. This paper focuses on discussing the contribution of the research to the development of the Communities of Practice framework for online learning. The discussion will review the main findings of the research, showing how these have led to the development of the theory. It offers an augmented framework, in which the elements of mutual engagement, joint enterprise and shared repertoire are enhanced to include those facets necessary to support an online learning com-munity. Finally, it is suggested that the augmented framework may have applicabil-ity to other professional groups engaging in online learning and working, with con-sideration given to how it might support e-based communities.

Keywords: Online learning, communities of practice, higher education, case study research

1 Introduction

The Communities of Practice (CoP) framework (Wenger 1998) was em-ployed as the theoretical underpinning for this doctoral study, which used a case study approach (Yin 1994) to consider whether students of the health care professions might develop online CoP as part of higher educa-tion study. This paper considers the theoretical basis of the learning model as a social and situated learning theory, reviewing the main components of community; mutual engagement, joint enterprise and shared repertoire. The application of the framework to online learning (OLL) contexts is considered, along with its use within this study. The discussion presents study findings, proposing an augmented framework that might be employed to support online learning.

2 Research context

This case study was centred in a higher education institution, drawing on a sample of final year nursing (adult, children's and mental health branches), radiography and radiotherapy students based within a faculty of health and social care. The faculty culture supports online learning, evidenced in its learning and teaching strategy, investment in a team of technical and design staff to support e-learning development and a staff development programme including authoring, implementation and supporting e-based delivery. Within the final year undergraduate pre-registration curriculum, an Interprofessional module (IP3) forms a compulsory component for nursing and allied health profession students, studying towards either a diploma (nurses) or honours degree (nurses and allied health professions). With the exception of a face-to-face introductory session, the entire module is supported online within the Blackboard virtual learning environment (VLE). Using a constructivist approach to enquiry-based learning, groups of up to eight students work with a facilitator to address an initial trigger question (see Hughes et al 2004). Over a period of eight weeks the students engage in online discussions through the discussion board and virtual classroom, submitting individual work online throughout the module and providing peer feedback that contributes to the final module assessment.

3 Theoretical basis

Lave and Wenger (1991) initially espoused learning as a situated activity, employing the phrase, 'Legitimate Peripheral Participation'. Learners were seen to participate in a community of practitioners and are assimilated into the socio-cultural practices of the community, gaining competence through knowledge and skill development acquired from those positioned as masters (Lave and Wenger 1991). This view of learning resurrected a model of apprenticeship and work-related learning that was developed as a social learning framework to include four components: community, identity, meaning and practice (Wenger 1998). Meaning is described as participation and reification, which is historically and contextually bound, constitut-

ing learning from negotiated experience and participation in the community. Practice, learning as doing, involves participation with the community,
with the aim of achieving shared goals. Reification, through the use of objects, shapes experiences and contributes to identity formation, with identity seen as learning as becoming. Community is then referred to as learning as belonging, where the community is the learning context and has
three essential components; mutual engagement, joint enterprise and
shared repertoire.

The model is also viewed as a situated learning theory as it describes learning in social and situated contexts, especially in the workplace (Fowler and
Mayes 1999, Fox 2000, Warhurst 2003). Indeed, Lave and Wenger (1991)
articulate a view of situated learning as 'an integral and inseparable aspect
of social practice' (p.31), which is captured in their descriptions of 'Legitimate Peripheral Participation.' Fowler and Mayes (1999) suggest this view
of situated learning is social anthropological, where a wide social context is
expounded and the CoP emphasises the relationship of the practitioner
with members of the CoP, which ultimately shapes the individual's identity.
This concurs with the views of Brown and Duguid (2002) who suggest situated learning is 'knowing how to be in practice', rather than 'knowing
about practice' (p.138), and thus involves a process of identity development for the newcomer through participation in the practice of the community

4   Theory: Research underpinnings

The development of the theory was based on five studies of apprenticeship
discussed by Lave and Wenger (1991). These included midwives in Mexico,
Vai and Gola tailors in Liberia, quartermasters in the United States of
America (USA), supermarket butchers in the USA and Alcoholics Anony-
mous (AA). Jordan's (1989) study of Yucatec midwives described family
tradition as the basis of learning. Midwifery was part of daily life for young
girls, observing and listening to stories from mothers and grandmothers
until they were able to deliver babies and act as competent midwives
themselves. Formal teaching was not central to the learning, but participation was the way of learning the art and science of midwifery. Lave and
Wenger (1991) comment on the variation seen in the forms of apprenticeship studied, where the tailors had a formal sponsored relationship with
their masters, quartermasters and butchers follow training programmes

and the membership of AA developed through demonstrated commitment to the community.

Becoming a member of a CoP involves learner engagement with the social processes of the community and its tools of the trade or artefacts. Developing competence in knowledge and skill is important in identity formation of the newcomer, who becomes part of the reproductive cycle of the CoP. This position seems to support commonality rather than diversity within the CoP, and has led to some criticism of CoP aiming to perpetuate communities (Eraut, 2003), rather than supporting growth and change.

5   Community dimensions

Wenger's (1998) conceptual framework sees practice as central to the community, as it is through practice that relationships are formed and identities are developed. There are three dimensions described as essential to a community (Wenger 1998); mutual engagement, joint enterprise and shared repertoire. This research explored whether such dimensions were evident in an online environment, where the community was composed of students working virtually. Mutual engagement is the basis for relationships necessary to the functioning of the CoP. It involves regular interaction of the members, who negotiate meaning of practice within the community. The practice does not reside in artefacts, though may employ computers or books. This interaction might be through formal meetings or informal exchange, which can enable engagement and act to maintain the community. Within an online community, engagement will require online communication and ongoing maintenance through e-mail, discussion boards and virtual classrooms. Wenger (1998) goes on to suggest communities are not homogenous, but are composed of diverse individuals, yet through working together they will influence each other's functioning within the community. Individuals will create their own identities that function within the community through mutual engagement, a sharing of practice.

The students involved in this study are members of different professional communities, nursing, radiography and radiotherapy, though are expected to work within an interprofessional community, where they make complementary contributions in caring for patients. Mutual engagement will require sharing of their understanding of professional practice and the creation of relationships between the members that can work to the benefit of the community and its patients. It is anticipated that the community would not necessarily live in harmony, but that there can be disagreement and conflict, yet there is concern that if commonality is favoured, this may limit diversity and conflict may be ignored.

Joint enterprise refers to a process that maintains the existence of the CoP. It is not merely about sharing goals, but a negotiated enterprise, involving mutual accountability (Wenger 1998). In an OLL context, this would require students negotiating ways of working towards communally agreed enterprise, within the constraints of an OLL environment. This does not mean all the students must share the same view, but must negotiate their enterprise. Negotiating joint enterprise manifests relations of mutual accountability within the CoP. Working in a mutually accountable way would require a conscious concern about their engagement with OLL. There should be a sense of responsibility as individuals and as a community, with members working to the benefit of the CoP and with concern for themselves and other members. Mutual accountability might be reified by ground rules set by the students at the start of the module, assessment goals to be achieved and limitations of the VLE. Shared repertoire might include developed routines, language, ways of working and stories within the practice of the community, generated through negotiating meaning (Wenger 1998). It is thought to include aspects of participation and reification. Actions and artefacts have histories of interpretation though it is suggested that they do not constrain meaning, but allow negotiation of new meaning and dynamic development through sustained engagement in the community. This aspect of a CoP tends to suggest longevity. Indeed, Fowler and Mayes (1999) feel CoP have a long term and stable perspective to them, which might restrict their use in more transient learning environments. It should be noted however, that research by Rogers (2000) discussed later, was conducted during a three-week online course and suggested the dimensions of a CoP were present.

6   Communities of practice in on-line learning

The development of a community of online learners working collaboratively within a constructivist-learning environment is discussed within the literature (see Palloff and Pratt 1999, Garrison and Anderson 2003), yet not all students seem to confirm the development of such a community of learning. Orey et al (2003) in the USA report the findings of interviews with participants of an OLL course. Limited by the very small sample of two males and one female, they describe interactions with coaches external to the learning group, engaging with them rather than forming a community of learners with tutors or fellow students.

Earlier ethnographic research by Spitler and Gallivan (1999) also in the USA, employed Lave and Wenger's (1991) 'Legitimate Peripheral Participation,' to consider how knowledge workers learnt their job within a firm of management consultants, also exploring the role of IT in learning. Thirty formal staff interviews and observations recorded evidence of mentorship and the importance of learning on the job, suggesting CoP had a significance influence on knowledge workers within this isolated example. Somekh and Pearson (2000) used Wenger's (1998) framework to analyse a European research project group linked by electronic communication and occasional face-to-face meetings, considering children's representation of information and communication technology (ICT). Presentation of the findings at conference revealed the CoP did not function easily when reliant on electronic communication. Dispersed working confounded the negotiation of joint enterprise; agreed deadlines were frequently missed as they failed to register in people's consciousness. Sharing a work environment would seem to act as a reminder of deadlines, an impetus missing from electronically linked communities. Shared repertoires and histories of the research partners also created tensions in negotiating a shared understanding of the research approach used, action research. This meant mutual engagement was undermined, as negotiated meaning remained illusive.

Rogers (2000), also in the USA, employed a case study methodology in applying the CoP framework to an online educational setting, providing the only previous example of such an application in the current literature. Though the study was limited by recruiting a small sample of 26 teachers and administrators participating in a three-week workshop 'Teachers of English as a Second or Other Language,' it offered an analysis of online dialogue. Rogers completed pattern matching and identified elements of the theory, though offers no independent verification of this analysis, an acknowledged weakness of the study. He confirmed the need for further research, whilst concluding the presence of collaborative working and identified Wenger's concepts of mutual engagement, joint enterprise and shared repertoire in the data. Wegerif (1998) proposed Lave and Wenger's (1991) framework of 'Legitimate Peripheral Participation' could be used to illuminate the relationship seen in a study of 21 Open University students studying online, between social dimensions of learning and success in a teaching and learning course. A constructivist pedagogy underpinned the course, which Wegerif (1998) felt was supported through developing a sense of community in the group of learners, seeing social processes as imperative to collaborative learning. Millen and Muller (2001) also in the USA, present research with designers and journalists where knowledge sharing in a CoP was situated in virtual and physical worlds. They highlighted the importance of web-masters and discussion-group moderators in nurturing an online CoP. More recently in the United Kingdom (UK), Murray (2003) describes the possibilities of developing online CoP through engagement in formal e-learning or informal environments. He comments on the potential advantages to nurses forming virtual CoP, referencing an earlier PhD (Murray 2002), for exploring practice, information exchange and potential practice development.

7   Research methodology

In order to address the main research question, 'How do the essential characteristics of a Community of Practice develop in higher education online learning environments?' a case study approach (Yin 1994) was adopted. This included two phases, that followed ethical approval gained through the University and faculty ethics committees and piloting of the data collection tools. Firstly, a questionnaire was employed to gain information about the characteristics of the student group (n=109), exploring gender, age, and previous computer use for learning and perceived confidence in use. In so doing it reflected a number of issues related to computer use identified in the literature (Boyle and Wambach 2001, Barrett and Lally 1999). Descriptive analysis of the questionnaire identified frequencies of response and supported the identification of the sample used in the second phase that included three data collection strands. The sample included both males and females, aged between 18 and 49, accessing computers from home, university and other sites. Representing the different branches of nursing, radiography and radiotherapy, they also presented perceived differences in confidence levels in computer use and reported various levels of experience of OLL.

8

As part of the second phase, seven students were grouped and consented to allow collection and analysis of their discussion board data across the six weeks of the module delivery (327 postings in total). Five students were asked to complete weekly online diaries and three students were interviewed after completion of the module. The data was analysed using a form of pattern-matching (Yin 1994), employing a matrix of categories identified from Wenger's framework (1998), as an approach to data analysis suggested by Miles and Huberman (1994). The data was analysed by matching verbatim and text data to the categories.

8 Research findings

The data suggests that some students were able to develop elements of mutual engagement, joint enterprise and shared repertoire. Students of the healthcare professions were therefore able to develop the essential characteristics of a CoP in higher education online learning environments, though this was not uniformly seen and a number of issues peculiar to online CoP emerged.

8.1 Mutual engagement

Mutual engagement was facilitated in a number of groups, with formal discussion and social discourse seen. Early engagement is viewed as important to online learning and teaching (Salmon 2004). Online exchange did however hold limitations, and the groups tended to use the virtual classroom to support negotiation and decision-making. Access issues were also evident. These resulted from technical problems as reported in other research (Gillis et al 2000) and a lack of IT skills amongst some students. Those without computer and Internet facilities at home were unable to benefit from the flexibility and convenience that online learning is reported to offer (Martyr 1998, Andrusyszyn et al 1999, Geibert 2000, Atack 2003).

'Me and computers do not mix, having written this for the second time because it crashed on me!!' (DipHE Adult nurse)

'I think I lost nearly two stone walking to Uni, that's the biggest advantage of online learning. HA HA HA.' (DipHE Adult nurse)

There was evidence that professional and personal identities were defined online, though a lack of physical presence in the learning environment resulted in problems in identity recognition for some. Assumptions were made about the composition of the group and there were claims from those students interviewed, that they had presented themselves differently online than they would in a face-to-face learning environment.

'Wow! I would never have guessed that English was not your first language.'(BSc Radiography)

'At the start of a classroom experience I would have been quieter. With this I felt I had to go on at the start and say, "hello, this is me!" and get on with it.' (BSc Child nurse)

8.2 Joint enterprise

Joint enterprise was again evidenced, though the degree to which this occurred varied, with some students feeling this was not achieved. Ryan et al (1999) found the immediacy of classroom delivery was important in comparisons with web-based delivery. Students in the study missed the immediacy of face-to-face interaction, particularly when the groups were trying to negotiate endeavour.

'They used the virtual classroom to discuss the guidelines. It was clear it was going to need a lot of negotiation.' (BSc Child nurse)

There were mixed accounts of group interactions, with some implying students were too polite, unable to disagree and negotiate, whereas other students reported open disagreement and strong negotiation in their groups. Acceptance of accountability for group endeavours also varied, with some students seeming to avoid commitment to their group, preferring to pursue autonomous working.

'People appear to be extremely polite when speaking over the Internet and I wonder if this is going to interfere with getting down to the nitty gritty of what we actually have to achieve.' (BSc Radiotherapy)

'I do feel that I haven't had much group interaction at all from this module.' (BSc Adult nurse)

'As I mentioned earlier, there only seem to be myself and two others who are pulling our weight!' (DipHE Mental Health nurse)

Technical issues and skills, as previously seen (Ragoonaden and Bordeleau 2000), may have adversely affected the engagement of students in online learning. It is suggested that differing technological skills affect group collaboration (Ge et al 2000). A lack of trust amongst group members can contribute to difficulties in-group functioning (Wegerif 1998, Murphy et al 2000). Individuals can also be reluctant to engage in online groups (Brown 2001). A perceived lack of time for engagement may also be an inhibiting factor (Conole et al 2002).

8.3 Shared repertoire

It is postulated that OLL environments with a brief existence may not have the longevity required to develop shared repertoire (Fowler and Mayes 1999). Attempts to review this are compounded by the difficulties of accessing evidence of routines, language, and ways of working online. Despite these concerns, a number of students had reached new understandings of interprofessional working and of IT skills, developed through community engagement.

'I learnt more about the other professions, especially radiotherapy.'(Dip HE adult nurse)

Some support for the development of shared repertoire resultant from online group learning is therefore evident. There was evidence of humour, shared discourse and some presentation of shared routines online.

'Thanks for saying hi the other day on the video conferencing. My class was wondering what was going on!!!'(Dip HE adult nurse)

in reply : 'Ahhh just tell em you're me toy boy' (BSc Adult nurse)

This was not uniformly developed however; with a number of students claiming autonomous working and learning had dominated their experience.

> '*We didn't discuss a lot in my group and I tended to get on with it.*'
> (BSc Child nurse)

Autonomous working can be the preference of students working in online groups, which it is suggested can particularly be the case if collaborative elements of online learning are not seen as relevant or focussed on assessment (Ragoonaden and Bordeleau 2000). The findings offer the potential to develop Wenger's (1998) framework, expanding it for use in OLL environments. Aspects of the social learning model and the three essential components of community are being reviewed to include those factors requiring consideration when applying the framework to OLL contexts.

9   Theoretical framework development

Uniquely this research has considered whether students of the healthcare professions could create an online CoP as part of a web-based learning experience. Its focus on the three components of essential for community functioning; mutual engagement, joint enterprise and shared repertoire, have led to the discovery of emergent issues to inform the development of online communities.

9.1   Developing mutual engagement

The student community working in a virtual environment needs to overcome access issues not normally present in a physically located CoP. To support mutual engagement the CoP members required IT skills and resources, both hardware and software, to engage in the virtual community. The study also found students required access to all components of the VLE, using the virtual classroom for synchronous discussion (real time interactive communication), crucial at times when the members were required to make decisions. On these occasions more 'instant' communication than that offered through asynchronous (not real time) vehicles such as the discussion board or email, was essential. These findings suggest that an online community will need to ensure participants have the technological provision and necessary IT skills to support engagement.

9.2 Developing joint enterprise

The students were able to present and develop individual identities online as part of joint enterprise. Professional identities of the healthcare students were shared and understandings of professional roles were enhanced. However, data also exposed the potential for identities to remain hidden. Examples included the presentation of gender and culture that could remain illusive to fellow community members. Additionally, students confirmed that their presentation online differed from that offered in the face-to-face learning environment, creating different personas. The emergence of different online personas, originally presented by Turkle (1997), suggested alternative identities could be portrayed in an environment where individuals might remain hidden. The interview data in particular suggested students felt communication online was curtailed due to word-processing difficulties. This hampered the openness of communication, resultant in a feeling that they were presenting different personalities online. There was also evidence of individuals failing to engage in community endeavour, with some students very obviously preferring to work autonomously.

9.3 Developing shared repertoire

Identifying elements of shared repertoire proved problematic in the analysis of the online environment, which lacked the richness that might be observed in a physically located CoP, where presentations of gestures, nuances, routines, stories are manifest. Additionally, IP3 lacked longevity, which seemed to lessen the opportunities for the development of shared understanding. It was clear however, that engagement in the OLL environment supported the development of IT skills amongst many students, with noted development in the use of various components of the VLE. The data also demonstrated IP learning, with a number of students discovering more about other healthcare professions from fellow community members. As the case study is limited to one group, it is difficult to know whether this learning was a feature particular to this group or whether this might be seen in other cohorts of students studying IP3.

9.4 An augmented framework

In developing Wenger's (1998) dimensions of CoP for the online environment due cognisance of the above facets needed consideration. The development and augmentation of the framework provided by Wenger (1998, p.73) is shown in figure 1.

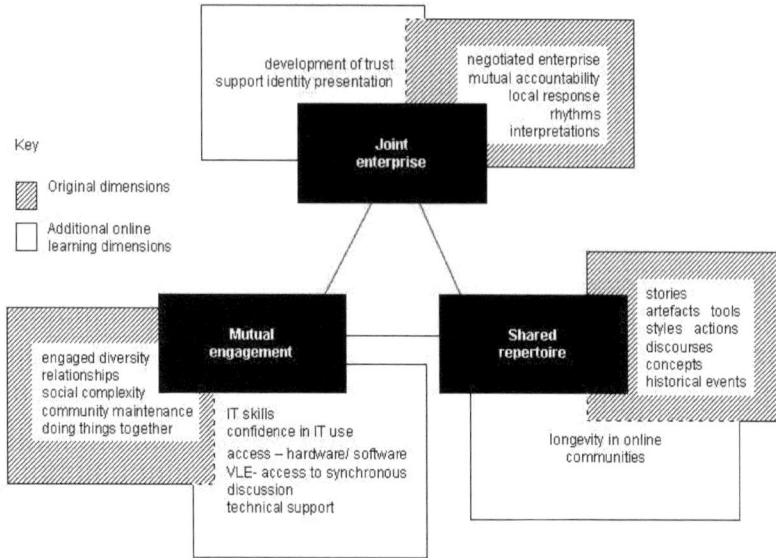

Figure 1: Augmented theoretical framework. *Adapted from Wenger 1998:78*

It presents the additional facets required of the CoP framework when applied to online environments. The model includes the three main components arranged in a structure that adapts Wenger's (1998) original presentation, with mutual engagement, joint enterprise and shared repertoire being positioned with the key facets related to each outlined in a 'square'. The model has been augmented to include the addition of a second 'square' to include the additional facets required within an online CoP. Mutual engagement includes; IT skills, confidence in IT use, access to computer hardware and software, VLE access and technical support. Joint enterprise sees the development of trust and support of identity presentation as an added facet of online community working, with shared repertoire suggesting longevity of the community is required. The additional 'squares' are attached using interrupted lines to depict the possibility of the CoP continuing to exist in physical environments, not requiring the online facets. The structure also offers scope for the online facets to support physically located contexts as well. For example, development of trust, whilst identified as important to the OLL CoP, is likely to impact on a physically located CoP.

10 Conclusion

The results of this study suggest that nursing, radiography and radiotherapy students learning online were able to demonstrate the development of mutual engagement, joint enterprise and shared repertoire, as elements of Community of Practice. This was not uniform and issues associated with operating in an online community enabled the identification of the additional facets required to support such communities, as presented in the augmented framework. The findings also raise ongoing concerns of interest to e-learning proponents and implementers. These relate to enabling access to the environment and supporting the development of computing skills. Issues of course design are also raised, requiring the linking of activities to assessment processes that necessitate the involvement of all members. Course design should ideally require students to explore each other's histories and values, limiting different persona presentation. Course longevity should also be considered. Despite these issues it is suggested that creating online communities of practice will allow the transcendence of geographical boundaries amongst learners, as seen with this interprofessional group of healthcare students. It has the potential to facilitate nationally and internationally based pursuit of academic endeavour and practice development.

A further publication by this author on this subject can be found at Moule P (2006) E-learning for healthcare students: developing the communities of practice framework. Journal of Advanced Nursing. 54 (3), 370-380.

References

Andrusyszyn, M. Iwasiw, C. and Goldenberg, D. (1999) Computer conferencing in graduate nursing education: Perceptions of students and faculty. The Journal of Continuing Education in Nursing. 30 (6), pp272-278

Atack, L. (2003) Becoming a web-based learner: registered nurses' experiences. Journal of Advanced Nursing. 44 (3), pp289-297

Barrett, E. and Lally, V. (1999) Gender differences in an on-line learning environment. Journal of Computer Assisted Learning. 15 (1), pp48-60

Boyle, D. and Wambach, K. (2001) Interaction in graduate nursing web-based instruction. Journal of Professional Nursing. 17 (3), pp128-134

Brown, H. (2001) Reflections on the development of a collaborative learning community for continuing professional development (CPD): The creative network. Higher Education Close Up Conference 2, Lancaster University, 16 July. http://www.leeds.ac.uk/educol/documents/00001744.doc Accessed 11 March 2003

Brown, J.S. and Duguid, P. (2002) The social life of information. Boston : Harvard Business School Press

Conole, G. Hall, M. and Smith, S. (2002) An evaluation of an online course for medical practitioners. Educational Technology and Society. 5 (3). http://ifets.ieee.org/periodical/vol_3_2002/conole.html Accessed 11 March 2003

Eraut, M. (2003) Editorial. Learning in Health and Social Care. 2 (3), pp117-122

Fowler, C. and Mayes, J. (1999) Learning relationships from theory to design. Association for Learning Technology Journal. 7 (3),pp 6-16

Fox, S. (2000) Communities of Practice, Foucault and Actor-Network Theory. Journal of Management Studies. 37 (6), pp853-867

Garrison, D. and Anderson, T. (2003) E-learning in the 21st century. A framework for research and practice. London : Routledge Falmer

Ge, X. Yamasiro, A. and Lee, J. (2000) Pre-class planning to scaffold students for online collaborative learning activities. Educational Technology and Society. 3 (3), 159-168. http://www.ifets.ieee.org/periodical/vol_3_2000/v_3_2000.html Accessed 11 March 2003

Geibert, R. (2000) Integrating Web-based instruction into a graduate nursing program taught via videoconferencing. Challenges and solutions. Computers in Nursing. 18 (1), pp26-34

Gillis, A. Jackson, W. Braid, A. MacDonald, P. and MacQuarrie, M. (2000) The learning needs and experiences of women using print-based and CD-ROM technology in nursing distance education. Journal of Distance Education. 15 (1), pp1-20

Hughes, M. Ventura, S. and Dando, M. (2004) On-line Interprofessional learning: introducing constructivism through enquiry-based learning and peer review. Journal of Interprofessional Care. 18 (3), pp263-268

Jordan, B. (1989) Cosmopolitan obstetrics: some insights from the training of traditional midwives. Social Science and Medicine. 28 (9), pp925-944

Lave, J. and Wenger, E. (1991) Situated learning: legitimate peripheral participation. Cambridge : Cambridge University Press

Martyr, P. (1998) Teaching a bachelor of nursing unit on-line: some experiences and results. The Australian Electronic Journal of Nursing Education. 3 (2), pp1-14. http://www.scu.edu.au/schools/nhcp/aejne/vol3-2/pjamartyrvol3_2.htm Accessed 6 March 2001

Miles, M. and Huberman, M. (1994) An expanded source book, qualitative data analysis. 2nd Edition. Thousand Oaks : Sage

Murphy, K. Mahoney, S. and Harvell, T. (2000) Role of contracts in enhancing community building in web courses. Educational Technology and Society. 3 (3), pp409-421. http:/www.ifets.ieee.org/periodical/vol_3_2000/v_3_2000.html Accessed 11 March 2003

Murray, P. (2002) Subject: talk to reflect-reflection and practice in nurses' computer-mediated communications. PhD thesis, The Open University, Milton Keynes, UK. http://www.peter-murray.net Accessed 30 January 2004

Murray, P. (2003) E-learning and its benefits for developing nursing practice. Paper presented at the IV International Congress of Medical Informatics, Havana, Cuba, 17-22 March, 2003. Information Technology in Nursing. 15 (2) pp18-24. http://www.bcsng.org.uk/itin15/VOL15-2res.pdf Accessed 13 February 2004

Orey, M. Koenecke, L. and Crozier, J. (2003) Learning communities via the internet à la epic learning: You can lead the horses to water, but you cannot get them to drink. Innovations in Education and Teaching International. 40 (30),pp 260-267

Palloff, R. and Pratt, K. (1999) Building learning communities in cyberspace. San Francisco : Jossey-Bass Publishers

Ragoonaden, K. and Bordeleau, P. (2000) Collaborative learning via the Internet. Educational Technology and Society. 3 (3), pp1-15. http://ifets.ieee.org/periodical/vol_3_2000/v_3_2000.html Accessed 11 March 2003

Rogers, J. (2000) Communities of practice: A framework for fostering co-herence in virtual learning communities. Educational Technology and Society. 3 (3), pp1-12. http://ifets.ieee.org/periodical/vol_3_2000/eo1.html Accessed 11 March 2003

Ryan, M. Carlton, K. and Ali, N. (1999) Evaluation of traditional classroom teaching methods versus course delivery via the world wide web. Journal of Nursing Education. 38 (6), pp272-277

Salmon, G. (2004) E-moderating: The key to teaching and learning online. 2nd Edition. London: Kogan Page

Somekh, B. and Pearson, M. (2000) Inter-cultural Learning arising from pan-European collaboration using electronic communications: sub-text or substance? Paper presented at British Educational Research Association Annual Conference, Cardiff, September

Spitler, V. and Gallivan, M. (1999) The role of information technology in the learning of knowledge work. New information technologies in organizational processes: field studies and theoretical reflections on the future of work IFIP-TC8-WG8.2 International Working Conference, pp257-275

Turkle, S. (1997) Life on the screen: Identity in the age of the Internet. New York : Touchstone Press

Warhurst, R. (2003) Learning to lecture: situating the knowing and learning of higher education teaching. Paper presented at British Educational Research Association Annual Conference, Edinburgh, September

Wegerif, R. (1998) The social dimension of asynchronous learning networks. The Journal of Asynchronous Learning Networks. 2 (1),pp 34-39

Wenger, E. (1998) Communities of Practice. Cambridge : Cambridge University Press

Yin, R. (1994) Case study research. Design and methods. 2nd Edition. London : Sage

Towards a Fusion of Formal and Informal Learning Environments: the Impact of the Read/Write Web

Richard Hall
De Montfort University, UK

Editorial Commentary

Web 2.0 applications allow a blending of formal and informal educational spaces which, as a modality, was simply unavailable as such 15 years ago. In this chapter Richard Hall proposes "fused" models of learning that embrace both physical and virtual worlds, formal and informal settings, individuals and communities ... a *Fused Learner Integration Model*. The originality of his work lies in the combination of these dimensions and the interconnections established between applications, content and people. He explores the *personal learning environment* (PLE) as a learning space offering new pedagogical and learning opportunities. PLEs are comprised of services and tools that allow one to shape his or her personal learning space as the learner aggregates, configures and manipulates digital artefacts in a manner that was barely defined a few years ago (Lubensky, 2006 ; Atwell, 2007). Today, PLEs are now a necessary complement to virtual learning environments (VLEs) (Henri et al., 2008). With the advent of Web 2.0, the movement toward PLEs is accelerating as they allow joining communities and sharing potential knowledge and learning spaces.

This paper highlights the added value of PLEs in terms of student control of a personal learning environment: individuals are autonomous in this regard (unlike their experience with institutional VLEs) and are thereby more in charge of their learning experience and able to diminish uncertainty. Proactive students also become producers of educational outputs and students are able to apply real life tools to their education. PLEs hold the promise of extending personal learning experiences beyond formal course activities.

Atwell, G. (2007). "Personal Learning Environment, The future of eLearning?" *eLearning Paper*, (2)1, pp.35-45

Henri, F, Charlier, B., and Limpens, F. (2008). "Understanding PLE as an Essential Component of the Learning Process." ED-Media, Society for Information Technology and Teacher Education International Conference *2008*, AACE, Chesapeake, 2008, pp. 3766-3770

Abstract: The read/write web or Web 2.0, offers ways for users to personalise their online existence, and to develop critical identities though the control of a range of tools. Exerting control enables users to forge new contexts, profiles and content through which to represent themselves, based upon user-centred, participative, social networking affordances of specific technologies. In turn these technologies enable learners to integrate their contexts, profiles and content in order to develop informal associations or communities of inquiry. Within educational contexts these tools enable spaces for learners to extend their formal learning into more informal places though the fusion of web-based tools into a task-oriented *personal learning environment*. Where students are empowered to make decisions about the tools that support their personal approaches to learning, they are able develop control over learning experiences and move towards their own subject-based mastery. Critically, they are able to define with whom to share their personal approaches, and how they can best connect the informal learning that occurs across their life to their formal, academic work. The personal definition or fusion of tools and tasks is afforded through individual control over the learning environment. The flowering of personal learning aims, mediated by technologies and rules of engagement, occurs within task-specific loops where learners can interpret and process epistemological signals. In turn, where those loops are located within broader, personalised environments students can make contextual sense of their learning and extend their own educational opportunities. Moreover, they can extend their academic decision-making through application in other contexts, and as a result manage their academic uncertainties. This is evidenced through a thematic study of the voices of both learners and tutors, which highlights how the read/write web can be used proactively by educators, using tasks to enable learners to fuse their informal and formal learning spaces, and thereby enhance their decision-making confidence. The structuring of learning spaces that enable users and social networks to manage educational processes is enhanced by read/write web approaches and tools, which in this paper is defined through a Fused Learner Integration model.

Keywords: learner; personal learning environment; formal learning; informal learning; read/write web; Web 2.0; thematic analysis

1 Introduction

The impact of the read/write web, or Web 2.0 as it is commonly known, on learner engagement within higher education is a central focus of current e-learning research (Ebner, Holzinger and Maurer, 2007; Conole et al., 2006; Mason and Rennie, 2007; Mayes, 2006). In particular, pedagogues have been re-thinking the implications of the read/write web in extending environments for situated, informal education, and for addressing the blurring of the boundaries between personal, social spaces and formal learning contexts (JISC, 2007).

In part, this blurring of spaces has been catalysed by the structures and affordances of user-centred technologies and their ability to be mashed (Webmashup.com, 2007) or modded (El-Nasr & Smith, 2006). The open nature and availability of key source code, wedded to the participative models that exist for re-working both content and presentation, enable dynamic, hybridised and derivative knowledge development. The ability for users to work with a variety of networks to mash-up, modify or recreate both content and applications extends their self-presentation and knowledge (Franklin and van Harmelen, 2007).

There is scope for extending this analysis to develop fused models of learning. Here users engage with both the signals and the connections that are made by-way-of real-time and synchronous engagements in the physical and virtual worlds (Ibrahim, 2008). This is connected to nascent work on both mixed reality (Mixed Reality Lab, 2008; MXR, 2008), where real-world and computer-generated information are merged to present new visualisations or simulations, *and* augmented reality (Hainich, 2006), where live visual streams are enhanced by computer-generated information. Critically, it is the fusion of information sources in the real and virtual worlds, primarily with or for users in similar contexts that affords new connections between formal and informal settings. Moreover, where fused, networked spaces are co-owned and developed, they enable users to engage varied perspectives and approaches (Barnett and Coate, 2007).

Empowering learners to design and deploy fused, formal and informal educational spaces not only extends the power of situated, individual, educational outcomes, but can also positively extend their personal learning experiences. This is impacted by: the contextual control available to users to manage uncertainty; the rules that underpin access and participation; the feedback and signals received from associations within those contexts; and the development of personal literacies. This thesis is framed by the outcomes of a thematic study of the voices of both learners and tutors, in order to argue that the read/write web should be used proactively by educators to enable learners to fuse their situated, informal and formal educational spaces, and thereby enhance the production of educational outputs.

2   Users, networks and the read/write web

The affordances of web-based applications are such that tools can be embedded within the curriculum at low cost in order to connect people and information. These tools are often known as Web 2.0 applications (O'Reilly, 2005), but they are also usefully referred to as read/write web applications. The use of the term 'read/write' emphasises an approach rather than a toolset and stresses the marriage of broadcast and interactive tools within a personalisable environment.

These applications afford opportunities for: social networking, using software like Facebook and Ning.com; social bookmarking, using tools like del.icio.us and Ma.gnolia; user-generated content, using blog and wiki software; virtual representation in worlds like Second Life; the syndication of content including multimedia; and innovative approaches to content and application-handling, including mash-ups and aggregation. Their impact has prompted practitioners to re-evaluate curriculum delivery, if not yet its design, and Sharpe (2006, p. 16) has highlighted that:

> This shift creates an era of opportunity for education. At the heart of education and learning lie the encounters that an individual has with people, places and things, and the opportunity each encounter presents for interaction, challenge and growth. As digital technology pervades everything around us, we can enrich each encounter to harness the global resources of the information world and of learning communities, to make it more appropriate in that moment to that individual.

These connections are catalysed by the interplay between applications, content and people. They produce signals and feedback between users within broader associational or friendship networks, and help to shape online beliefs, identities and, importantly, decision-making and agency (Hall, 2008). Anderson (2007) has highlighted six key areas in which these connections between applications and users are made real: user-generated content; the power of the crowd; data on an epic scale; an architecture that supports participation; network effects; and openness in content and computer code. The openness and malleability of use of these tools empowers users to express themselves to others, and to take part in shared activities, in a variety of contexts.

The ways in which the structures of these technologies allow their application and their content to be repurposed enables socially-constructed, dynamic, hybridised and derivative knowledge to be developed. The processes of producing mash-ups and modifications to applications can be seen in both technical and cognitive terms (El-Nasr & Smith, 2006; Webmashup.com, 2007). Through the control of code that is open source or open standards, and through the integration of media presented in multiple applications, individuals have the opportunity to rethink the spaces and places in which they represent themselves (Hodgson and Reynolds, 2005; Franklin and van Harmelen, 2007). Through the reframing of individual and collective tools and artefacts an understanding of the world and a view of difference can be generated.

There are still many issues for read/write web participants to consider, around: identity presentation and formation; engagement, agency and marginalisation; privacy and security; and developing technological confidence. Anderson (2007, p. 53) pinpoints 'the need to explore further the informal, social aspects of the learning that takes place and the many issues concerning participation. We cannot, for example, assume everyone is happy working in the "self-publish" mode.' However, our engagement with read/write web tools and experiences forms part of an agenda for educational change, through the development of new spaces and contexts for enriching formal education through informal activities (Goodfellow and Lea, 2007; HEA, 2008).

3   Informal and formal education: the affordances of the read/write web

A critical space for individual learning development to occur is a formal learning environment. Eraut (2000, p. 12) defines such contexts as consisting of: a prescribed learning framework or schedule; specified learning tasks; facilitation by a professional educator; and formal accreditation, based upon external specifications. Where the rules that underpin activity in these places are framed by tutors and learners, they can enhance levels of personalisation and ownership, underpinned by personal self-reliance. In terms of technologies, institutionalised formal learning is defined by a standard toolkit, like a virtual learning environment that interoperates with institutional administrative databases, for instance student record systems. In this way, individual and group interactions and assessments can be captured, monitored and assured. The key here is that personalisation is achieved through accredited frameworks delivered in professional settings (DIUS, 2008).

The concept of informal education is contested although many would use the following terms in its description: education "owned" and "directed" by the learner; independent study; non-formally timetabled education; education using non-institutional technologies; and engaging learning that takes place away from traditional, educational contexts. The interface between traditional and non-traditional contexts or spaces has come more sharply into focus through the use of emergent read/write web and mobile technologies, which emphasise learning linked to ownership, context, personalisation and differentiated tasks (HEA, 2008). Critically, these tasks and spaces have different rules from traditional academic contexts, even if they are less structured and more open (Barnett, 2008). With users operating in multiple spaces, there are widespread affordances for personal validation, the formation of new allegiances, freeing access to varied resources, and achieving self-reliance through critical action across the boundaries of networks. Moreover, these networks and contexts are at once virtual and real.

In defining an approach to informal education Leadbeater (2000, p. 112) has argued that:

Schools and universities should become more like hubs of learning, within the community, capable of extending into the community... More learning needs to be done at home, in offices and kitchens, in the contexts where knowledge is deployed to solve problems and add value to people's lives

The development of added value occurs through self-education, and through both membership of formal educational classes *and* associations with informal, external networks of people (McGiveney, 1999). Increasingly, it is the critical ability that an individual learner develops in fusing their formal and informal learning, which levers educational gains (Joseph Rowntree Foundation, 2007). This personal fusion is supported by trusted peers or practitioners and enables users to seek out appropriate personal connections between spaces, so that signals can be passed between networks, to inform action.

This provokes strategic and operational issues for higher education providers about:
- curriculum design, delivery and assessment;
- enhancing personal, technological access and participation;
- the development and ownership of personalised learning environments (PLE);
- the impact on institutional strategies for learning and teaching, estates, IT, staff development and library services; and
- the impact on staff-student and student-student relationships.

In developing strategies to manage these issues, education providers and practitioners need to address issues around control of the learning environments that they support, and enabling connections to be forged and fused with informal learning spaces.

4   Fused learning spaces
Developing the connections between formal and informal networks and spaces moves us towards an acceptance of a personalisation and ownership of the learning process that coalesces within a range of spaces, networks and applications. In this way, there is the hope that learners can develop agile agency in deploying new learning or literacies, within new

contexts, and as a result enhance their outcomes. This is driven by the motivation and engagement of the learner within what can be termed fused spaces.

Fused, personal environments consist of a 'diverse range of possible technologies and applications' in both virtual and real worlds (Ibrahim, 2008, p.1), which are interconnected and enable proactive, personalised actions to be taken. They emerge from fused media, which 'can facilitate context-aware, situation-aware, multi-scale, proactive, and sign/signal-action dynamics in real time' (Fused Media Lab, 2008). Such actions are driven by closed-loop models where action is impacted by contextual, environmental triggers and a dynamic understanding of human behaviour. The connections that are fused between triggers, environment and behaviours enable signals to be passed between a user and a socio-technical system. By making sense of these signals, systems and users can learn from new experiences, better predict future outcomes and make better decisions.

In a read/write web world, this approach appears blurred by a mashing of identities and networks, within and across a multitude of spaces for sending and receiving signals. However, for specific tasks or outcomes, users make sense of their collected, personal spaces and networks, in order to perform closed-loop operations that are closely linked to real-time tasks. Ibrahim (2008, p.2) notes that these operations in both physical and virtual contexts 'can best be described as the fusion of worlds'. In extending these closed-loop, task-based strategies one can pick out the key elements of Ibrahim's fused framework that impact upon networks or spaces for personal, learning development, namely:

- A defined "focus aspect", like a personal aim or need;
- The provision of personalised signals and feedback mechanisms through interactive, social media that enable users to regulate their actions and development;
- Personal mastery over new resources, networks or literacies, which promote certainty; and
- Social or networked rules or frameworks that enable the robust management of uncertainty, whilst enabling a dynamic engagement with change.

In the fusing process, open applications and networks are connected technologically and cognitively by the individual to provide a place for action and identity formation. The most important element is the impact of feedback and signals that are passed between an individual and both their preferred media forms and their networks (Boekaerts et al., 2005). The feedback loops that occur empower users to construct ways of acting (Nicol and Macfarlane-Dick, 2006; Vygotsky, 1978), and thereby to confront and control their uncertainty about working within academic cultures, or engaging with academic tasks, or evaluating and creating academic content. Where such uncertainties are controlled or made certain, this activity positively reinforces a user's actions or decision-making processes (Barnett, 2008).

This fusion of educational spaces is itself impacted by the role of technologies. There is increasing evidence that e-learning is rarely seen as separate or special by learners and that academically they are deploying a mix of personal and institutional technologies over which they have more choice, access and control (JISC, 2007). The JISC LXP project (2007) argued that there is an increasing complexity and blurring of boundaries between the formal and informal use of technologies. In turn this facilitates advanced networking and the development of new critical literacies. As Jeffs and Smith (1990) note, separate learning environments are viewed in different ways, depending upon the information and people who operate within them, and the relationships that are formed between those 'resources' and a particular user.

In the fusing process, open applications and networks are connected physically and cognitively by the individual to provide augmented places for action and identity formation (Mixed Reality Lab, 2008). This does not produce a simulated reality; rather it enables the user to engage with real uncertainties, through participation with tasks and feedback loops. For instance, students on placement might experience enhanced project work using mobile devices and social networks. Equally, networks of users might fuse hardware, media and content to produce shared stories. The most important element is the impact of feedback and signals that are passed between an individual and both their preferred, mixed media forms and their social networks. These have the potential to augment ubiquitous, experiential learning (Educause, 2005), and empower users to construct ways of acting (Vygotsky, 1978), and thereby to confront and control uncertainty. Where uncertainty is controlled or made certain, it positively reinforces a user's actions or decision-making processes (Bandura, 1977). The ways in which a user can fuse informal and formal personal resources, networks and literacies underpins their assemblage of a meaningful PLE.

5 Assemblage of fused personal learning environments

The Ravensbourne Learner Integration project (JISC, 2008a) argues that a PLE is 'a learning environment that is assembled through learner choice'. It encompasses the personalised aggregation of tools, networks and content from a range of formal and informal places. This aggregation can exist in several places or be presented in one space, depending upon the nature of the personal tasks to be undertaken, or the specific aim to be achieved. In this way the learning context, and both the learning that takes place and the artefacts that are produced within it, are owned and controlled by the individual student, rather than the institution. The read/write web underpins this approach by dint of its user-centred, participative and networked affordances (Anderson, 2007).

The interactions between an individual and their environment lead to reciprocal determinism, ensuring that both individual and environment are changed. In this model, learning is a combination of watching, thinking and trying (Kolb and Fry, 1975). When a person succeeds in a task s/he becomes more confident and more willing to take on new operations. The situated nature of this practice is highlighted by Tennant (1999, p. 170), who stresses how expert knowledge and skill can be gained from everyday social experiences at work, and in community or family, and how personal mastery can be forged through goal-directed behaviour with appropriate feedback.

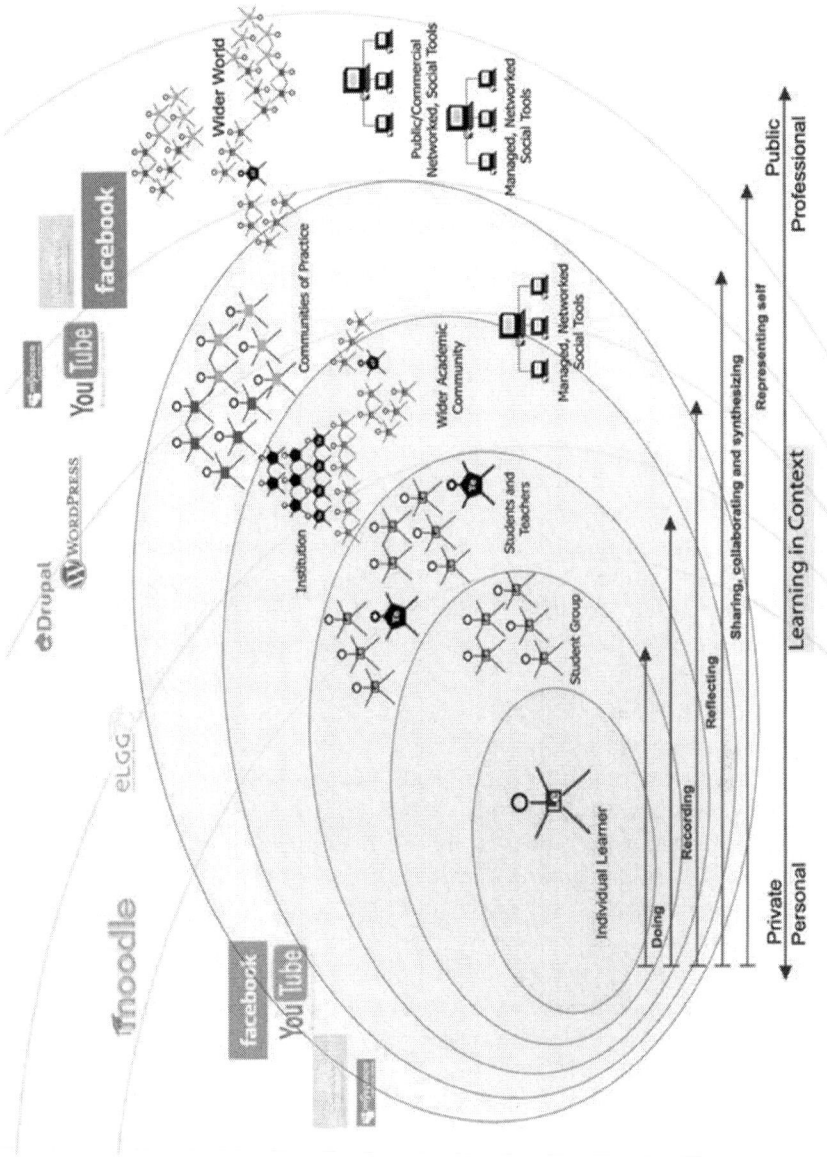

Figure 1: e-Learning in context, the Ravensbourne Learner Integration model

Given the growing impact of read/write web technologies on educational processes, it is important to evaluate the personal impact of social tools in a range of formal and informal settings, in order to develop a critical understanding of how PLEs are assembled and fused in specific domains.

The PLE offers us a complex view of learning environments based upon differentiated user needs (JISC, 2008b). The Ravensbourne Learner Integration project (JISC, 2008a) has developed an assemblage model that focuses upon the individual's transition from private to public learning in the context of social software and communities of practice.

The Learner Integration model is important because it highlights the links between: personal mastery in specific domains; social learning in communities or associations of practice; and social media and technologies. It highlights how self-education and critical literacy are enhanced through active participation with user-centred media and within groups that make sense to the individual. This frames a constructivist paradigm where learners can situate themselves, in order to make and record actions, to reflect on those actions, to share decisions and thoughts with others, and to represent aspects of their identity within validated networks.

Defined environments for learning are unique to each learner based on their learning aims. Moreover, they are fused from specific formal and informal associations using social media, where meaningful, rule-based signals can be processed into action. Therefore, the context surrounding the Learner Integration model is enhanced through Ibrahim's (2008) fused framework. By integrating and making explicit the elements that focus upon the development of the learner's focus aim, her/his signal processing and network rules, Ibrahim's (2008) fourth theme relating to personal ways of managing uncertainty and anxiety can be addressed. Thus, it is possible to refine the technological, social and cognitive links made by the individual in overcoming uncertainty and developing mastery. This accords with the view of Illich (1971, pp. 77-8) that the key question is not 'what should someone learn?' but 'what kinds of things and people might learners want to be in contact with in order to learn?'

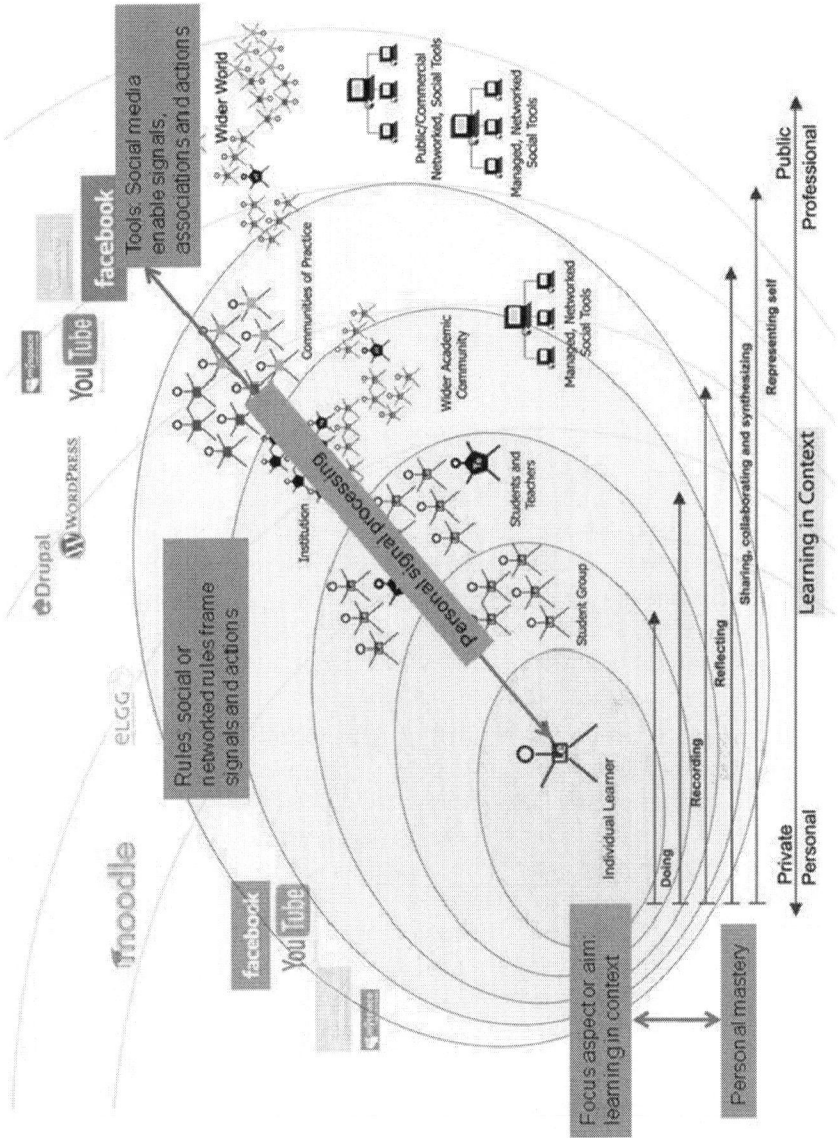

Figure 2: e-Learning in context, a Fused Learner Integration model

For Illich education was owned by the individual in becoming a self-aware actor, and he also argued (1977, p. 31) that the questions individuals are empowered to ask coupled to the socio-technical tools available to them, supports personal emancipation. The read/write web affords tools for encouraging individuals to associate with each other in contexts that support doing, questioning and re-conceptualising (Siemens, 2008). Linking the four strands of the fused learning spaces framework into the Learner Integration model scaffolds an adaptive, environmentally-flexible toolset that furthers participation though personally-focused activity.

Individual students can develop their own approaches to conceptual mastery, and in the process of successfully modelling their learning they are able to overcome academic uncertainty. Such modelling is underpinned by their proximity to formal and informal associations, which are personally meaningful in enabling a learning aim or focus aspect to be achieved (Siemens, 2008). In turn the rules and frameworks that are negotiated within these networks, associations and communities frame a fused learning space for making environmental sense of signals and feedback. Therefore, evaluating the personal, fused spaces in which users operate and produce is critical in understanding how the read/write web offers opportunities to extend learning opportunities in higher education.

6   A note on context and evaluation

The discussion that follows pivots around the impact on the development of fused personal learning environments of deploying read/write technologies within one UK university. The evaluation is designed to analyse conversations about emergent curriculum approaches, in order to examine how the tools provided are being embedded, and to align that view with student expectations. It focuses upon the triangulation of two data sources.

- Student evaluations: in-depth interviews and on-line focus groups with 129 students at all levels, including postgraduate, in all five University faculties between 2005-08; and
- Staff evaluations: in-depth interviews with 11 staff before, during and after they introduced read/write technologies into their curricula.

The evaluator did not focus conversations upon the implications of the read/write web for developing PLEs. Rather, the approach engaged with understanding the systematic implementation of e-learning innovations and their impact on learning and teaching, in order to support the critical, reflective, accountable, self-evaluative and participative improvement of practice (Zuber-Skerritt 1992, pp. 14-17). Thematic content analysis was used in order to unpick and capture the emergent themes from the interviews. The interviews were conducted and the coding scheme was framed and tested by the same evaluator in order to maintain an internal consistency of approach. The coding scheme was iterated over time using two separate samples of ten interviews, and tested by a peer working in a clinical psychology context (Boyatzis, 1998; Joffe and Yardley, 2004).Thus, this latitudinal evaluation examines what students say about the impact of the read/write web on their learning experiences, in order to provide a pragmatic description of their expectations for the use of those tools and approaches in the curriculum (Reason and Bradbury, 2001). This accords with the view of Reason (2003, 106) that the 'fundamental strategy of action research is to 'open communicative space' and help the emergence of 'communities of inquiry'.' This approach becomes rigorous through consensual participation. As Elliott (2007, p. 159) has noted: 'the democratic process of enquiry determines... which descriptions of the human environment, natural as well social, best enable human beings effectively to interact with it to satisfy their needs and desires.' (Elliot, 2007, p. 161).

7 Emergent outcomes

The conversations with students and staff about the read/write web were designed to test assumptions about the personalised use of these tools. However, only a subset of interviews developed in directions whereby a dialogue could open up and be classified in terms of the Learner Integration model or the developmental aspects of the fused model. As such, appropriate themes emerged from the categorisation of what students and staff themselves said about its broader influence on their learning and teaching. This categorisation of conversations with students pivoted around their discussion or use of specific terms or foci that can be interpreted to signify particular themes. Those which are captured in table 1 are those with the highest frequency.

Table 1: Themes from interviews and focus groups with students in 2005-08 on their experiences of e-learning in the curriculum (129 interviewees)

	Number
Outcomes 1: personal ways of managing uncertainty through contextual control [aligned with the Tools of the Fused Learner Integration model]	
A focus on personal boundaries for an environment: use of terms like 'involvement', 'conversations' and 'agreement'	45
A focus on personal control of tools: discussion of terms like open access technologies, variance of use and shared communication	71
Outcomes 2: networked rules for access and participation [aligned with the Rules of the Fused Learner Integration model]	
A focus on dialogue between networks of learners-as-peers, and learners-with-tutors	39
A focus on aspects of access and participation between networks of learners-as-peers, and learners-with-tutors	62
Outcomes 3: interpreting signals through associations [aligned with the Personal signal processing of the Fused Learner Integration model]	
A focus on the impact of collaboration through technologies on specific academic tasks	44
A focus upon feedback on specific academic tasks, supported by technologies	49
Outcomes 4: towards a focus aim of critical literacy [aligned with the Focus aim and Personal mastery of the Fused Learner Integration model]	
A focus on personal domain-specific learning outcomes	65
A focus on personal ontological outcomes	32

In the scoping discussion that follows, each of these themes is linked to the perceptions of eleven staff as elicited from detailed conversations with them about innovation in the curriculum. It should be noted that the evaluator found no differences on these themes: across subject areas; between distance and local learners, or between undergraduates and postgraduates.

Outcomes 1: personal ways of managing uncertainty through contextual control

A focus on who sets the boundaries for a learning context is linked to who controls the types of tools that can be used therein. The control of the connections between formal and informal education is a personal enabler. One level two student noted that 'staff define the use of technologies and students expect to be told what to do'. The programme tutor believed that this was because 'they don't come in with enough ideas, but I would like this to change over time, that they talk to each other, in MSN etc. and share thoughts and values'. However, for those students who raised issues around control and ownership, a passive view was not the norm, for instance a distance learning student argued that 'I feel like we are penalised by being forced to attend [face-to-face] sessions rather than building our own independence and autonomy and authority in the workplace'. A level three undergraduate concurred arguing that 'an integrated system is the way forward – something that allows the academic and social functionality to be personalised... I think it is important to apply real-life tools to education.'

In part student expectations for more control of their learning environment are shaped by their agency and confidence in relation to the tasks and tools at hand. A first-year student argued that 'I'd like spaces to work together with people I know. I don't want to make a fool of myself with people I don't know.' Understanding the point of a tool contextualised by a learning task requires facilitated deliberation amongst a cohort, which enables students to find 'the right place' for the use of web-based tools. A third-year student had a mature view on this issue and stated 'I like personalised tools, web media, animations, YouTube and that, and I like feeds that connect them like my Firefox toolbar that has good navigation based upon my thought processes and preferences.'

Personal contextual preferences also impacted upon views of staff engagement in student-led spaces. One learner commented that 'Teachers can join Facebook, and if we ran a group maybe they could just see a small portion of your page, rather than all of your personal and professional life.' For some staff, student control of the use of non-institutional, read/write tools, and their subsequent impact on formal learning was problematic. One felt that 'many staff feel threatened and challenged by technological innovation that widens student aspirations'. A second tutor added perceptively that 'the students have discovered and use web-based [tools] – they are migrating themselves into industry toolsets. We need to adapt.' This adaptive view was also held by a student representative who argued that 'this normally explicit division between the academic and the social spaces could easily become blurred with use of Web 2.0, and therefore learners must understand where boundaries should be placed to ring-fence both the personal and academic experience these tools offer.'

Outcomes 2: networked rules for access and participation

The critical theme of negotiated rules for access and participation within curriculum groups emerged from the student interviews. One learner 'liked the fact that group pages were only seen by us and no-one else, and I can find out what the other group members are contributing to the work. We can then decide who to send information to.' For some students access and participation stemmed from the personal efficacy of tools that could be used both formally and informally. A level one learner highlighted that subscription was a critical means of access to the curriculum: 'not everyone will have iPhones and video or audio, but most text, and can subscribe to stuff. That way I could get critical announcements and reminders.' This places value upon a curriculum that connects individual ways of working to a personal ability to access adaptive tools and strategies.

For some cohorts of students, the use of tools outside the control of the teaching team was critical in building a rationale for access and participation. One postgraduate argued that 'we built the community between us and now I am less apprehensive about getting feedback. It removed the fear of isolation.' This was echoed by a second postgraduate: 'we need social engagement and debates about practice. In the end we set up our own MSN chat room to move to total ownership of our learning.' Both students felt that the differences between group members were overcome by a shared participation in a defined learning context.

This proactive strategy for connecting learning contexts using different read/write tools was not uniform. One level two tutor argued that this mindset takes time to emerge and that these read/write tools would affect 'participation in the formation of their own project [group] identity, [and] it will be interesting to see how this affects their overall sociability'. This

Richard Hall

type of participation, within a context that respects the differences between students and fosters a space for personal action, was echoed by a separate lecturer:

> *The Web2.0 software is 'owned' and editable by them, and they can see what each other have done and all are free to comment... what staff say has to be encouraging and of value, emotionally, technically, educationally, within a set of guidelines that promote active interest.*

The level of active interest, facilitated by local environmental control and participation, is spurred by personal proximity to relevant networks and associations.

Outcomes 3: interpreting signals through associations
Most curriculum interactions are fixed within institutionalised spaces. However, for some students external associations with validated others hold most value. One level two student drew these matters together:

> *I use Web 2.0 technologies because it is an interest thing. I am able to say 'I found this and what do you think?' It is a process of self-validation, to have opinions outside [the University]. I want an external view, a wider opinion on my work. This is not what people are taught, but outside experience is important in practice.*

For a sub-set of students the ability to manage their work through dialogue with non-institutional networks is critical in their own reflexive assessment of personal progress. A second, level two learner noted that 'I don't want a closed view. Making my work more abstract is important – my identity is defined externally and I like to go off on my own and work with others. I like [our use of read/write tools] as it is an extension of my way of working.' This sense of shared, open validation was important for one programme team: 'We encourage students to share their resources with others via wikis, del.icio.us, and other open applications.' This demonstrates a mastery over the intended curriculum outcomes and develops trust and validity in the production of personal and social assets.

37

Thus, a complex set of approaches exists in the fusion of informal and formal learning contexts enhanced by the interpretation of signals. A distance learner using synchronous classrooms noted how they 'are a good community building tool with opportunities for us to learn in teams, allowing you to gather knowledge and experience and ideas quickly and share it'. However, a level one student highlighted that the extension of personal skills in virtual worlds, like Second Life, was forged out of shared interests between wider groups of people. He noted that

> *the first thing we did was explore places that looked good and where people had already solved the problems we had. We talked to them about this about how they had solved problems. They talked to us because we were using the same language, and they could get something from us.*

One of his peers went on to argue that this impacted his creativity: 'I can understand the programming but it is the creative side that has changed, because I have had to work outside our normal group.'

This demonstrates the strength of associations based upon common interests in promoting mastery and conceptual understanding, through signal processing and trusted feedback. These associations are underpinned by personal control over the deployment of read/write technologies. A student in a different cohort noted that 'We all have MySpace sites – they are more interactive and I can get to know people or even get constructive feedback from strangers. If someone has an opinion it's great; it's simple and I get to re-think my space.' For one tutor this crystallised around the value of 'exposure to the use of technologies in a variety of creative and discursive ways... the students do understand the tools and know about the issues.'

Outcomes 4: towards a focus aim of critical literacy
Developing association and participation, in negotiated informal and formal educational spaces, can enhance critical literacy. One learner highlighted how she valued 'the ability to hear other people's views and have the opportunity to express mine' but that 'I would like to see more collaboration between lecturers and students in order to make learning more in-

teresting'. The process of sharing and modelling practice helped students manage curriculum anxieties, as one second-level lecturer highlighted:

> *The Web 2.0 software is 'owned' and editable by them, and they can see what each other have done and all are free to comment... what staff say has to be encouraging and of value, emotionally, technically, educationally, within a set of guidelines that promote active interest.*

The level of active interest, facilitated by local environmental control and participation, spurs critical thinking, and the development of collaborative strategies for managing uncertainty.

Situated support was seen as vital in enabling learners to enhance their educational experiences. A first-year student argued 'I accept that we need to move to total ownership of our learning but we still expect a graduated level of support throughout.' A peer agreed and highlighted that in developing critical literacy in a particular subject area 'our ownership of blogging tasks means that we have to get used to tagging and linking and thinking like this'. A level two tutor concurred with the use of these tools for personal ownership, arguing that 'the better students had a quality and depth of notes that went beyond a set text to produce more original thinking that was linked to a topic of personal interest. They took time to personalise their case studies.'

A separate postgraduate student highlighted the value in extending their academic writing of blogging: 'There is a much more relaxed feel about writing a blog, it's much more natural and still has the potential to raise one's writing ability.' This learner went on to argue that informal, reflective writing enhanced her critical engagement in structured teaching sessions: 'You have to read and discover and discuss these in the tutorials and so the blog complements and summarises points.' For this learner, the experience of discovery through read/write web tools helped to fuse formal and informal educational literacies and enhance her subject-specific mastery over time. This longer-term approach was reiterated by a level three student: 'I like the idea of constantly updating [the blog], so you have to think about it and develop personal ideas over time.'

However, for some students simply having access to a personalised tech-nological space is an issue in developing critical literacy. One first-year stu-dent noted that 'next year we will have broadband in the flat – it was the first thing we organised. Last year we didn't have broadband and I was [disappointed]. It is a necessity when you are at university, especially as the library is [busy] at assessment times.' These issues of technological access and marginalisation mean that universities cannot presume that all of their students are able to enhance their learning in a wide range of in-formal and formal educational networks. Managing the impact of techno-logical uncertainty and anxiety on curriculum disenfranchisement is critical for higher education.

8 Conclusion

The read/write web offers ways for users to personalise their online exis-tence, and to develop their own critical identities. User centred, participa-tive, social networking tools enable learners to create informal associations or communities of practice, in which to develop their own subject-based mastery. By fusing web-based tools into a task-oriented PLE, students gain control over their learning experiences. Moreover, they are able to define who they share those experiences with, and to connect their informal edu-cational lives to their formal, institutional work.This fusion is a product of control in four key areas.

- A defined "focus aspect", like a personal aim or need;
- The provision of personalised signals and feedback mechanisms through interactive, social media that enable users to regulate their actions and development;
- Personal mastery over new resources, networks or literacies, which promote certainty; and
- Social or networked rules or frameworks that enable the robust management of uncertainty, whilst enabling a dynamic engage-ment with change.

The structuring of personal learning spaces that enable users or social networks to manage these four areas is enhanced by read/write web ap-proaches and tools, and can be modeled through an extension of the Ravensbourne Learner Integration model. This Fused Learner Integration model highlights the impact of personal aims, tools and rules, within closed, task-specific loops that enable signal processing to take place. In this way, one can begin to see how students can make contextual sense of their learning, develop their own approaches to mastery and extend their own learning opportunities. By utilizing these applications and their ways of working, formal and informal educational spaces can be fused, in order positively to extend participation and the development of critical literacy. As a student representative highlighted 'It is important for the learner to have control over the tools they use and to make informed choices about how to use them.' The contextual control available to learners in personalising their own learning environments, their modes of access and participation within multiple networks, and the associations that are made in those contexts enable those learners to overcome uncertainty. In this way, the read/write web can proactively shape the means for the production of educational outputs through its affordances for the creation of fused learning spaces.

References

Anderson, P. (2007) *What is Web2.0? Ideas, technologies and implications education*, [online] Report for UK Joint Information Systems Committee, Available: http://www.jisc.ac.uk/media/documents/techwatch/tsw0701.pdf [26 September 2008].

Bandura, A. (1977) *Social Learning Theory*, New York: General Learning Press.

Barnett, R. (2008) *A Will To Learn: Being a Student in an Age of Uncertainty*, Buckingham: Society for Research into Higher Education/Open University Press.

Barnett, R. and Coate K. (2005) *Engaging the curriculum in higher education,* Maidenhead: McGraw-Hill.

Boekaerts, M., Pintrich, P. and Zeidner, M. (2005) *Handbook of self-regulation,* San Diego: Academic Press.

Boyatzis, R.E. (1998) *Transforming Qualitative Information: Thematic Analysis and Code Development*, Thousand Oaks, California: Sage.

Conole, G., de Laat, M., Dillon, T. and Darby, J. (2006) *JISC LXP Student experiences of technologies: Final report*, [online] UK Joint Information Systems Committee, Available: http://www.jisc.ac.uk/media/documents/programmes/elearning_peda

gogy/lxp%20project%20final%20report%20dec%2006.pdf [26 September 2008].

Department for Innovation, Universities and Skills (2008) *Informal Adult Learning - Shaping The Way Ahead*, [online], Available: http://www.adultlearningconsultation.org.uk/ [26 September 2008].

Ebner, M., Holzinger, A. and Maurer. H. (2007) 'Web 2.0 technology: Future interfaces for technology enhanced learning?' *Lecture Notes in Computer Science*, vol. 4556, pp. 559-68.

Educause (2005), 7 *things you should know about Augmented Reality*, [online], Available: http://www.educause.edu/ir/library/pdf/ELI7007.pdf [26 September 2008].

El-Nasr, M.S, and Smith, B.K. (2006) *'Learning through game modding'*, *Computers in Entertainment*, vol. 4, no. 1, article 7, [online], Available: http://portal.acm.org/citation.cfm?id=1111293.1111301&coll=GUIDE&dl=GUIDE&idx=J912&part=magazine&WantType=Magazines&title=Computers%20in%20Entertainment%20%28CIE%29&CFID=35405541&CFTOKEN=43280928 [26 September 2008].

Elliott, J. (2007) 'Educational research as a form of democratic rationality', in Bridges, D. and Smith, R.D. [eds] *Philosophy, methodology and educational research,*. London: Blackwell.

Eraut, M. (2000) 'Non-formal learning, implicit learning and tacit knowledge in professional work', in Coffield, F. (ed.) *The Necessity of Informal Learning*, Bristol: The Policy Press.

Franklin, T. & van Harmelen, M. (2007) *Web 2.0 for content for learning and teaching in higher education*, [onine] Report for UK Joint Information Systems Committee. Available: http://www.jisc.ac.uk/media/documents/programmes/digitalrepositories/web2-content-learning-and-teaching.pdf [26 September 2008].

Fused Media Lab (2008) *Fused-Media Lab... digital-economy innovation*, [online], Available: http://www.cse.dmu.ac.uk/~ibrahim/FML.htm [26 September 2008].

Goodfellow, R. and Lea, M.R. (2007) *Challenging e-learning in the university*, Buckingham: Society for Research into Higher Education/Open University Press.

Hainich, R. (2nd Edition, 2006) *The End of Hardware: A Novel Approach to Augmented Reality*, Charleston: Booksurge.

Hall, R. (2008) 'The impact of the read/write web on learner agency', *e-Learning*, forthcoming.

Higher Education Academy (2008) *Learning from Digital Natives Project*, [online], Available: http://www.academy.gcal.ac.uk/ldn/ [26 September 2008].

Hodgson, V. and Reynolds, M. (2005) 'Consensus, difference and "multiple communities" in networked learning', *Studies in Higher Education*, vol. 30, no. 1, pp. 11–24.

Ibrahim, M.K. (2008) 'A Generic Architectural Framework for Proactive Systems Inspired by Molecular Biology', *Proceedings of the 2nd IEEE International Systems Conference*, pp. 1-8. Available at: http://www.ieeexplore.ieee.org/iel5/4509976/4518971/04519024.pdf ?isnumber=4518971&prod=STD&arnumber=4519024&arnumber=4519024&arSt=1&ared=8&arAuthor=Ibrahim%2C+Mohammad+K [26 September 2008].

Illich, I. (1971) *Deschooling society,* London: Calder and Boyars.

Illich, I. (1977) 'Disabling professions', in ibid. [ed.] *Disabling professions*, London: Marion Boyars.

Jeffs, T. and Smith, M. (eds) (1990) *Using Informal Education,* Buckingham: Open University Press.

Joint Information Systems Committee (2007) *In their own words: Exploring the learner's perspective on e-learning*, [online], Available: http://www.jisc.ac.uk/media/documents/programmes/elearningpedagogy/iowfinal.pdf [26 September 2008].

Joint Information Systems Committee (2008a), *Ravensbourne Learner Integration Project*, [online], Available: http://confluence.rave.ac.uk/confluence/display/SCIRCLINR/Home [26 September 2008].

Joint Information Systems Committee (2008b), *The CETIS Personal Learning Environments Blog*, [online], Available: http://zope.cetis.ac.uk/members/ple [26 September 2008].

Joffe, H. and Yardley, L. (2004) 'Content and Thematic Analysis', in Yardley, L. and Marks, D.F. [eds] *Research Methods for Clinical and Health Psychology,* London: Sage.

Joseph Rowntree Foundation (2007) *Experiences of poverty and educational disadvantage*, [online]. Available:

http://www.jrf.org.uk/knowledge/findings/socialpolicy/2123.asp [26 September 2008].

Kolb. D. A. and Fry, R. (1975) 'Toward an applied theory of experiential learning', in Cooper, C. (ed.) *Theories of Group Process,* London: John Wiley.

Leadbeater, C. (2000) *Living on Thin Air. The new economy,* London: Penguin.

Mason, R. and Rennie F. (2007) 'Using web 2.0 for learning in the community', *The Internet and Higher Education*, vol. 10, no. 3, pp. 196-203.

Mayes, T. (2006) *JISC e-learning models desk study. Stage 2: Learner-centred pedagogy: Individual differences between learners,* [online], Report for UK Joint Information Systems Committee. Available: http://www.jisc.ac.uk/uploaded_documents/Stage%202%20Learning%20Styles%20(Version%201).pdf [26 September 2008].

McGiveney, V. (1999) *Informal Learning in the Community. A trigger for change and development,* Leicester: NIACE.

Mixed Reality Lab (2008), T*he Mixed Reality Laboratory,* [online], Available: http://www.mrl.nott.ac.uk/ [26 September 2008].

MXR (2008) *Mixed Reality Lab,* [online], Available: http://www.mixedrealitylab.org/ [26 September 2008].

Nicol, D. and Macfarlane-Dick, D. (2006) 'Formative assessment and self-regulated learning: A model and seven principles of good feedback practice', *Studies in Higher Education*, 31(2), 199-218.

O'Reilly, T. (2005) 'What is web 2.0? Design patterns and business models for the next generation of software', [online], Available: http://www.oreillynet.com/pub/a/oreilly/tim/news/2005/09/30/what-is-web-20.html [26 September 2008].

Reason, P. (2003) 'Pragmatist philosophy and action research: Readings and conversation with Richard Rorty', *Action Research*, vol. 1, pp. 103-23.

Reason, P. and Bradbury, H. (eds) (2001) *Handbook of action research*: *Participative inquiry and practice,* London: Sage.

Sharpe, B. (2006) The Ambient Web, in *Emerging technologies for learning,* [online], Review by the British Educational Communications and Technology Agency, Available: http://partners.becta.org.uk/upload-dir/downloads/page_documents/research/emerging_technologies.pdf [26 September 2008].

Siemens, G. (2008) New structures and spaces of learning: The systemic impact of connective knowledge, connectivism, and networked learning [online], Available: http://elearnspace.org/Articles/systemic_impact.htm [26 September 2008]

Tennant, M. (1999) 'Is learning transferable?' in Boud, D. and Garrick, J. (eds.) *Understanding Learning at Work*, London: Routledge.

Vygotsky, L.S. (1978) *Mind and society: The development of higher psychological processes* Cambridge, MA: Harvard University Press.

Webmashup.com (2007) *The Open Directory for Mashups & Web 2.0 Mashup APIs,* [online], Available: http://www.webmashup.com/ [26 September 2008].

Zuber-Skerritt, O. (1992) *Action research in higher education.* London: Kogan Page.

Engaging the YouTube Google-Eyed Generation: Strategies for Using Web 2.0 in Teaching and Learning

Peter Duffy
The Hong Kong Polytechnic University, Hong Kong

Editorial commentary

This paper offers a very operational review of Web 2.0 tools in educational contexts and specifically, Duffy examines three student-centric tools in depth – blogs, YouTube and wikis – that can be created by students or controlled by professors. Duffy argues the need to change course designs to incorporate Web 2.0 technologies because the habits, customs and codes of Millennium and X Generation students differ from those of previous generations. But he goes further, arguing that educational systems must evolve from "Push" to "Pull" education (Richardson, 2005). For professors, this implies new pedagogies that require a certain level of courage, because proposing blogs, wikis or YouTube learning activities is, for many professionals, less comfortable than traditional PowerPoint content delivery. It requires trust in the process, the tools and the participants. Once these fundamentals are incorporated, 2.0 tools offer great learning opportunities.

In terms of best practice for *blogs*, Duffy refers to reflexive writing (a new dynamic in teaching rhetorical sensitivity and reflection) that promotes critical and creative thinking. Audet (2010) similarly applauds the metacognition power of blogs as this modality allows personal journals and *learning stories* to be developed by students and thus implicates metacognitive processes. He suggests that best practices for *YouTube* include fragmenting videos within learning activities (using pause, sound off, note taking, cuts, etc.) to avoid "virtual library" situations while enhancing the "community" aspect of video sharing. Best practice for *wikis* includes collaborative annotated bibliographies, group authoring and other community-centric productions: building a wiki is an on-going student process favoring communal constructivism (Holmes et al., 2010).

Holmes, B., Tangney, B., Fitzgibbon, N, A., Savage, T, & Mehan, S. (2001). *Communal Constructivism: Students constructing learning for as well as with others.* Centre for Research in IT in Education Trinity College Dublin, Irlande.
https://www.cs.tcd.ie/publications/tech-reports/reports.01/TCD-CS-2001-04.pdf
Audet, L. (2010). Wikis, blogues et Web 2.0 : Opportunités et impacts pour la formation à distance. Montréal, Canada : Réseau d'enseignement francophone à distance du Canada (REFAD).
http://refad.ca/nouveau/Wikis_blogues_et_Web_2_0.html

Abstract: YouTube, Podcasting, Blogs, Wikis and RSS are buzz words currently associated with the term Web 2.0 and represent a shifting pedagogical paradigm for the use of a new set of tools within education. The implication here is a possible shift from the basic archetypical vehicles used for (e)learning today (lecture notes, printed material, PowerPoint, websites, animation) towards a ubiquitous user-centric, user-content generated and user-guided experience. It is not sufficient to use online learning and teaching technologies simply for the delivery of content to students. A new "Learning Ecology" is present where these Web 2.0 technologies can be explored for collaborative and (co)creative purposes as well as for the critical assessment, evaluation and personalization of information. Web 2.0 technologies provide educators with many possibilities for engaging students in desirable practices such as collaborative content creation, peer assessment and motivation of students through innovative use of media. These can be used in the development of authentic learning tasks and enhance the learning experience. However in order for a new learning tool, be it print, multimedia, blog, podcast or video, to be adopted, educators must be able to conceptualize the possibilities for use within a concrete framework. This paper outlines some possible strategies for educators to incorporate the use of some of these Web 2.0 technologies into the student learning experience.

Keywords: Web 2.0, e-Learning, YouTube, blog, Wiki

1 Introduction

Why should the notion of incorporating Web 2.0 and interacting with for example socially distributed and user-created videos (e.g. from www.youtube.com) be important within education? In what ways has the rapid development of digital technologies associated with the term Web 2.0 and their use in education enabled individuals to interact differently within existing ecologies of learning? How can we as educators engage the YouTube, Google-eyed generation?

Students today have grown up within a world of pervasive technology including mobile phones, digital cameras and the omnipresent internet. Described as, "Gen-X, Millennials, the Nintendo and Net Generation" (Tapscott, 1997; Oblinger, 2003; Olsen, 2005), these students blog, play games in immersive 3-D worlds, listen to podcasts, instant message friends, listen to music, author their own video for www.youtube.com and collaborate on the creation of 'digital stories' for their ePortfolio. They absorb information quickly, in images and video as well as text, from multiple sources simultaneously. They operate at what Prensky (2004) describes as, "twitch speed", expecting instant responses and feedback. They prefer random "on-demand" access to media; expect to be in constant communication with their friends and ease of access in the creation of their own content.

In his article, Growing Up Digital: How the Web Changes Work, Education, and the Ways People Learn, John Seely Brown (2002) uses ecology as a metaphor to describe an environment for learning. Brown says, "An ecology is basically an open, complex adaptive system comprising elements that are dynamic and interdependent. One of the things that make an ecology so powerful and adaptable to new contexts is its diversity." Brown further describes a learning ecology as, "a collection of overlapping communities of interest (virtual), cross-pollinating with each other, constantly evolving, and largely self-organizing."

New Web 2.0 technologies and websites, such as a blog, wiki or YouTube, make new demands on learning, and they provide new supports to learning, even as they also dismantle some of the learning supports upon which education has depended in the past. If we agree that there are changes occurring across the learning ecology and, that new conceptualisations are required to use these emerging technologies, then some care should be taken to think deeply about the impacts of Web 2.0 on the processes and practices of pedagogy.

The focus of this paper will be on a pragmatic exploration of blogs, You-Tube and wikis as illustrative and typical examples of technologies and websites that reflect the changing landscape of our Web 2.0 learning ecology. Clearly, the choice of these three areas does not delimit the categorisation of Web 2.0 tools to only these three, and other areas such as Virtual Worlds / aka Second Life (http://www.secondlife.com/) or social sharing sites such as Face-book (http://www.facebook.com/) or, Myspace (http://www.myspace.com/),etc could be dealt with, however, by limiting the choice within this paper to an exploration of blogs, YouTube and wikis as illustrative of Web 2.0 it is envisaged that this will provide some starting frames of reference within which to consider strategies for using Web 2.0 within teaching and learning for the reader. Explored will initially be definitional aspects of Web 2.0 and a general understanding of Web 2.0 before delving into a detailed focus on some possible strategies for educators to incorporate the use of blogs, YouTube and wikis (as representational of Web 2.0) into the student learning experience.

2 A student context

Why would the notion of incorporating user-created videos (e.g. from www.youtube.com as one illustrative example of Web 2.0) be important within education? From a student perspective we must reflect on the changing nature of our students as key stakeholders in the educational process. Sometimes called "digital natives" or the "Nintendo generation", these new millennial's approach work, recreation and certainly education in new ways. (Tapscott, 1997) They absorb information quickly, in images and video as well as text, from multiple sources simultaneously. They operate at what Prensky (2004) describes as, "twitch speed", expecting instant responses and feedback. They prefer random "on-demand" access to media; expect to be in constant communication with their friends and ease of access in the creation of their own new media.

There is some debate about students' ability to transfer these technological 'real world' skills to an academic context (refer for example to The

ECAR Study of Undergraduate Students and Information Technology, re-
leased in December 2006. But certainly not debated is the dominance and
pervasive use of the technology by students. According to an American
study on teen content creators and consumers, (Lenhard & Madden,
2005), 57% of online teens create content for the Internet. That amounts
to half of all teens ages 12–17, or about 12 million youth. The study referred to students being involved in the following activities: create a blog;
create or work on a personal web-page; create or work on a webpage for
school, a friend, or an organization; share original content such as artwork,
photos, stories, or videos online; or remix content found online into a new
creation. In learning, these trends are manifest in what is sometimes called
"learner-centered" or "student-centered" design (Marzano, 2006). This is
however, more than an adaptation to accommodate different learning
styles or allowing the user to change the display of a website; it is the plac-
ing of the control of learning experience itself into the hands of the
learner. The phenomena of Web 2.0 provide for students an unprece-
dented way to access, socialize and co-create.

3   Web 2.0

"Web 2.0", a phrase coined by O'Reilly Media in 2003 (O'Reilly, 2005), refers to a perceived second generation of web-based interactions, applications and communities. It is considered to be inclusive of a shift from a
World Wide Web that is "read only" to a Web that is being described as
the "Read Write Web" (Gillmor, 2007). Instead of content that was for the
most part static, we are now seeing the ability to remix content in different
ways, in order to suit contextual needs. The Web is evolving to become
more like an area for social and idea networking. Students negotiate meanings and connections within Web 2.0 social spaces or idea networks, exchange bits of content, create new content, and collaborate in new ways.

The term Web 2.0 has been applied to a heterogeneous mix of the familiar
with the innovative and emergent and as such can be considered problematic in a definitional sense. What must be considered here though is not
the shifting ground in relation to definitional aspects of Web 2.0 but how
the term is defined for the purposes of this exploration of its use within
education and pedagogic possibilities? As Alexander, (2006, p.32) states,

"Ultimately, the label "Web 2.0" is far less important than the concepts, projects, and practices included in its scope".

Presented here are some broad characteristics of a Web 2.0 web-site in order to further delimit the term for the reader:
- "network as platform"; delivering (and allowing users to use) applications entirely through an internet browser
- users own the content on a site and exercise control over it
- an architecture of participation that encourages users to contribute
- a rich, interactive, user-friendly interface
- social-networking functions

In summary, O'Reilly (2005) indicates that "Web 2.0" stands for the idea that the Internet is evolving from a collection of static pages into a vehicle for software services, especially those that foster self-publishing, participation, and collaboration

User-centered Web 2.0 phenomena such as blogging, social video sharing (exemplified by YouTube) and collective editing (wiki or Wikipedia as an example) are disrupting traditional ideas about how students interact online and how content is generated, shared, and distributed. Presented next are some specific characteristics of blogs, YouTube and wikis as well as, educational benefits and strategies for the educational use of each.

3.1 Examples of Web 2.0

Tim O'Reilly (2005) provides a comparison between websites and functions that typically illustrate Web 1.0 and 2.0. In his initial brainstorming, he formulated the following examples and this initial list has been adapted to include some previous terms such as read-write web to provide further insight and a context for the reader in relation to these terms.

Some of the terms in Table 1 may be problematic for the novice Web 2.0 reader and so a brief description of some of the more common terms is provided. Blogs provide a personal commentary or news on a particular subject and many function as a personal online diary. A typical blog combines text, images, and links to other blogs and web media. The ability for readers to leave comments in an interactive format is an important part of many blogs. Blogging is content created from a personal point of view, in a personal voice.

Table 1: Comparison of Web 1.0 with Web 2.0

Web 1.0		Web 2.0
DoubleClick	-->	Google AdSense
Ofoto	-->	Flickr
Akamai	-->	BitTorrent
mp3.com	-->	Napster / Podcasting
Britannica Online	-->	Wikipedia
personal websites	-->	blogging
evite	-->	upcoming.org and EVDB
domain name speculation	-->	search engine optimization
page views	-->	cost per click
screen scraping	-->	web services
publishing	-->	participation
content management systems	-->	wikis
directories (taxonomy)	-->	tagging ("folksonomy")
stickiness	-->	RSS - syndication
Read Web	-->	Read-Write Web
Linear	-->	Non-Linear
Daily ME	-->	Daily WE
Old Media	-->	New Media / or Social Media

(This table has been adapted from http://www.oreillynet.com/pub/a/oreilly/tim/news/2005/09/30/what-is-web-20.html)

A wiki (sometimes wiki wiki) is a web application designed to allow multiple authors to add, remove, and edit content. (Cunningham and Leuf (2001). The multiple author capability of wikis makes them effective tools for mass collaborative authoring. Wikipedia, is one of the best known wikis. RSS, folksonomies and tagging are often part of the transformation to the "Read Write Web." The term folksonomy (derived from "folk" and "taxonomy") was coined by Thomas VanderWal (Vanderwal, 2006) and refers to a form of organic categorization that comes from internet users as they encounter new information. Podcasting, is the creation and distribution of an audio or more recently video recording online. It is distributed over the internet using RSS or syndication feeds and is often suitable for playback on portable players such as an iPod.

Various "social" new media sharing websites have become associated with the term Web 2.0 as well. Photo-sharing Web sites such as Flickr, (www.flickr.com) are becoming hubs for students sharing photos. In addition to being a popular Web site for users to share personal photographs, the service is widely used by bloggers as a photo repository. Its popularity has been fueled by its innovative online community tools that allow photos to be tagged and browsed by folksonomic means.Video-sharing web sites continue to proliferate on the internet. The article "The ultimate Online Video List", indicates 210 different online video sites. (refer to http://www.everybodygoto.com/2007/05/21/the-ultimate-online-video-list/). At present the website with the largest market share is www.youtube.com and it is this site that we will be focusing on in relation to new media and an exploration of specific strategies to use YouTube in teaching and learning.

3.2   What is a blog?

Paquet (2003) refers to the term, blog, initiated by Barger in 1997, as a log of the Web – or Weblog. In its simplest form it is a Website with dated entries, presented in reverse chronological order and published on the Internet. The word blog is both a noun and a verb. People who maintain a blog are called bloggers. The act of posting to a blog is called blogging and the distributed, collective, and interlinked world of blogging is the blogosphere.

3.2.1   *Characteristics of a blog*

A Weblog or blog can be described as an online journal with one or many contributors. Besides straight text and hyperlinks, many blogs incorporate other forms of media, such as images and video.

Blogs differ from traditional websites and provide many advantages over traditional sites, including:

- easy creation of new pages, since new data is entered into a blog usually through a simple form and then submitted with the blogger (or person adding the entry to the blog website) updating the blog with little or no technical background - blogs have thus become the novice's Web authoring tool;
- filtering of content for various blog entries, for example by date, category, author, or one of many other attributes;

- most blog platforms allow the blog administrator to invite and add other authors, whose permissions for creating content and access are easily managed;
- providing a personal writing space that is easy to use, sharable, and automatically archived;
- ability to link and inter-link to form learning communities;
- opportunity to serve as a digital portfolios of students' assignments and achievements;
- extensions into fully-featured content management systems

3.2.2   *Educational benefits of blogs*
Potential benefits as identified by learning specialists Fernette and Brock Eide and cited by Will Richardson (2006) in *Blogs, Wikis, Podcasts, and Other Powerful Webtools for Classroooms* include the following:

- can promote critical and analytical thinking;
- can promote creative, intuitive and associational thinking;
- (creative and associational thinking in relation to blogs being used as a brainstorming tool and also as a resource for interlinking, commenting on interlinked ideas);
- can promote analogical thinking;
- potential for increased access and exposure to quality information;
- combination of solitary and social interaction

Within the structure of a blog, students can demonstrate critical thinking, take creative risks, and make sophisticated use of language and design elements. In doing so, the students acquire creative, critical, communicative, and collaborative skills that may be useful to them in both scholarly and professional contexts. The growing popularity of blogs suggests the possibility that some of the work that students need to do in order to read well, respond critically, and write vigorously, might be accomplished under circumstances dramatically different from those currently utilized in education.

3.2.3   *Strategies for using blogs in teaching and learning*
The following are some possible uses of blogs in education:

Within a personal academic perspective a blog can support:
- reflection on teaching experiences;
- categorized descriptions of resources and methodologies for teaching;
- ramblings regarding professional challenges and teaching tips for other academics, and
- illustration of specific technology-related tips for other colleagues

Within an organizational perspective a blog can support:
- a common online presence for unit-related information such as calendars, events, assignments and resources, and an
- online area for students to post contact details and queries relating to assessment

Within a pedagogical perspective a blog can support:
- comments based on content, literature readings and student responses;
- a collaborative space for students to act as reviewers for course-related materials;
- images and reflections related to industry placement;
- an online gallery space for review of works, writings, etc., in progress, making use especially of the commenting feature;
- teachers encouraging reactions, reflections and ideas by commenting on their students' blogs, and
- the development of a student portfolio of work

3.3 Further questions to be explored

Consider asking your students how much reflective writing they do? Then, for comparison, ask them how much time they spend writing emails, using ICQ or MSN Messenger, and surfing the Internet? Most will be heavily involved in the latter. To the current generation of students, the Internet and other forms of electronic discourse are not necessarily associated with their concept of "reading and writing" in an educational sense, but rather are tools for social interaction. Blogging, as a socially driven public written reflection, can change the dynamic of teaching rhetorical sensitivity and reflection. Many students are already highly socially active in Internet-based environments, interacting with and commenting on one another's written materials – even without formally realising that they are doing so. The proclivity and popularity of Websites such as the video sharing site www.youtube.com and the blogging space www.blogger.com indicate a growing impetus towards personal expression and reflection, and the sharing of "personal "spaces.

3.4   What is YouTube?

YouTube is a popular video sharing website where users can upload, view, and share video clips. YouTube has become an enormously popular form of web 2.0 new media. A recent article in Wired cites an average of 65,000 uploads and 100 million videos viewed per day on YouTube (Godwin-Jones, 2007).

3.4.1   *Characteristics of YouTube*

A typical YouTube webpage is usually made up of the following components:

- the wide variety of video content including movie and TV clips and music videos, as well as amateur content such as video blogging and short original videos;
- unregistered users can watch most videos on the site; registered users have the ability to upload an unlimited number of videos;
- Flag – ability to indicate a video that has inappropriate content;
- Title - main title of the video;
- Tags – keywords specified by the person who has uploaded the video;
- Channels – relating to groupings of content;
- Related videos - determined by the title and tags, appear to the right of the video;
- Subscribe – registered users can subscribe to content feeds for a particular user or users;
- Comments – often not monitored can be provided by any registered user about a video uploaded;
- Views – the number of times a video has been watched;
- Rating - videos can be rated by registered users

3.4.2 Educational benefits of YouTube

Video can be a powerful educational and motivational tool. However, a great deal of the medium's power lies not in itself but in how it is used. Video is not an end in itself but a means toward achieving learning goals and objectives. Effective instructional video is not television-to-student instruction but rather teacher-to-student instruction, with video as a vehicle for discovery.

YouTube is increasingly being used by educators as a pedagogic resource for everything from newsworthy events from around the world to "slice-of-life" videos used to teach students within an ESL (English as a Second Language) course. From instructional videos to an online space to share student authored content.

Some general guidelines recommended by Clark and Mayer (2002) in relation to considering the appropriate use of any media to improve learning suggest that media must:

- be aligned with expected learning or performance outcome;
- reduce cognitive load;
- exclude superficial text or graphics;
- be appropriate for target learner's learning literacy

Educators (and students alike), will find that video is an effective catalyst and facilitator for classroom discourse and analysis.

3.4.3 Strategies for using YouTube in teaching and learning

Video can be a powerful educational and motivational tool. However, a great deal of the medium's power lies not in itself but in how it is used. Video is not an end in itself but a means toward achieving learning goals and objectives. Effective instructional video is not television-to-student instruction but rather teacher-to-student instruction, with video as a vehicle for discovery.

YouTube is increasingly being used by educators as a pedagogic resource for everything from newsworthy events from around the world to "slice-of-life" videos used to teach students within an ESL (English as a Second Language) course. From instructional videos to an online space to share student authored new media.

Some general guidelines recommended by Clark and Mayer (2002) in relation to considering the appropriate use of any media to improve learning suggest that media must:
- be aligned with expected learning or performance outcome
- reduce cognitive load
- exclude superficial text or graphics
- be appropriate for target learner's learning literacy

Video learning shouldn't be passive. These are some guidelines relating to the specific use of video to promote active viewing and maximize learning.

1. **SEGEMENT** - allow your students to watch the video in short segments.
2. **NOTES** - videos are ideal for developing note-taking skills. Take notes on the first viewing, then rewind, replay and check them. This can be done individually or collectively as a class discussion / brainstorming session.
3. **PAUSE** - Use the "pause" feature to temporarily stop the tape and allow your students to try to predict/recall what will happen next.
4. **SOUND OFF** - for video sequences that rely on visuals, turn the sound off and narrate. This technique works especially well for listing the steps of a process.
5. **PICTURE OFF** - use the audio clues to describe what is on screen. Compare and contrast the predictions with the actual video.
6. **PREVIEW** each video carefully to determine its suitability for the lesson's objectives and student's learning outcomes.
7. **INTEGRATE** the video into the overall learning experience by adding an experimental component to the lesson. Activities can be done prior to viewing: to set the stage, review, provide background information, identify new vocabulary words, or to introduce the topic. The activity can be done after viewing to reinforce, apply, or extend the information conveyed by the program. Often the video can serve as an introduction or motivator for the hands-on activity to come.

8. **CUT** – use online video editors like www.cuts.com or www.eyespot.com to capture the concepts that are most relevant for your lesson topic. It is often unnecessary and time-consuming to screen a program in its entirety. When previewing a program, look for segments particularly relevant or useful to the lesson or activity planned.

9. **FOCUS** - give students a specific responsibility while viewing. Introduce the video with a question, things to look for, unfamiliar vocabulary, or an activity that will make the program's content more clear or meaningful. By charging students with specific viewing responsibilities, teachers can keep students "on task" and direct the learning experience to the lesson's objectives. Be sure and follow-up during and after viewing the tape.

10. **AFTER** - when students have viewed the video consider: What interested them? What didn't they understand? How can you relate the program to their experiences and feelings? Ask the students to add comments / blog on the video. How can you validate and appreciate diverse reactions to the material?

Teachers and students alike will find that video is an effective catalyst and facilitator for classroom discourse and analysis. Coupled with hands-on learning, a new media, video-enhanced curriculum can be invaluable for expanding the learning experience and by incorporating a medium that is as popular, forceful and familiar; educators can tap into the existing enthusiasm towards this form of new media. (The above strategies were adapted from: http://www.idahoptv.org/ntti/strategies.html
and
http://www.edb.utexas.edu/fieldexp/SampleSeminars/SampleSeminar11.php)

Below are some specific examples of approaches to incorporating YouTube into the teaching and learning experience:

- YouTube can be used to create a learning community where everyone has a voice, anyone can contribute, and the value lies equally within the creation of the content and the networks of learners that form around content discovered and shared. (adapted from Educause Learning Initiative, 2006);

- allow your students to create a short video as part of an assessment item instead of the traditional essay. Becoming involved in
  the creation of a video, "heightens a student's visual literacy, an
  important skill in today's electronic culture" (Educause Learning
  Initiative, 2006);
- YouTube allows the learner to experiment in new media to convey
  information and knowledge. "Many educators believe that the act
  of creating content, in virtually any form, is a valuable learning
  exercise" (Educause Learning Initiative, 2006);
- record a video of a guest presenter relevant to your content and
  use the YouTube comments feature to generate some discussion;
- pose a question at the end of class that can be considered from
  distinct viewpoints and ask your students to search for 2-3 video
  references relating to the different perspectives. The use of video
  as a part of an anticipatory set to promote discussion can be useful tool to engage with an audience already enamoured with the
  YouTube phenomenon;
- the use of video also has several advantages over graphic and textual media. E.g.: portrayal of concepts involving motion, the al-
  teration of space and time; the observation of dangerous processes in a safe environment; dramatization of historical and complex events; demonstration of sequential processes the viewer
  can pause and review (Misanchuk, Schwier & Boling, 1996);
- to support language learning, at the end of one of your classes,
  decide on a particular topic and ask your students to search for
  short videos on this topic to watch it and create a difficult vocabulary guide;
- ask students to capture a series of video vignettes related to their
  work placement. This will provide a rich authentic resource both
  for current students and future use. One example this are the
  video vignettes described within Diane Skiba's (2007) article,
  "Nursing Education 2.0 via YouTube;
- within higher education Jenkins, (2007) describes the 'YouNiversity' and suggests an intellectual network where students interact
  not only with professors, but with industry and the community;
- YouTube can be used as a virtual library to support classroom lectures by providing students with access to video clips. (Conway,
  2006)

3.4.4   Further questions to be explored

YouTube is not necessary for good teaching, in the same way that wheeling a VCR into the classroom is not necessary. Within an examination of Web 2.0 sites such as YouTube and the discourses that frame their use educators should consider: how do we engage with these Web 2.0 technologies, and how do we teach students to think critically about their potential uses? How do video sharing sites such as YouTube reshape our participation in and out of the classroom? Such questions, of course, do not have simple answers. It is suggested that educators need to go beyond treating video sharing sites as only virtual libraries and instead emphasize the features more aligned with Web 2.0 such as the role of social comments, video responses to existing content, flexible possibilities for collaborative assessment and other features of media sharing collaboration.

3.5   What is a Wiki?

A wiki is a group of Web pages that allows users to add content, similar to a discussion forum or blog, but also permits others (sometimes completely unrestrictedly) to edit the content (Arreguin, 2004). What distinguishes wikis from blogs, discussion fora, or other content management systems is that there is no inherent structure hard-coded: wiki pages can be interconnected and organized as required, and are not presented by default in a reverse-chronological, taxonomic-hierarchical, or any other predetermined order. In essence, the wiki offers a vast simplification of the process of creating HTML pages, and thus is a very effective way to build and exchange information through collaborative effort.

3.5.1   Characteristics of a Wiki

The following are some typical characteristics of Wikis:

- where a blog is (usually) the writings of one person to be read by many, a wiki is a website that allows a user to add content, but also allows that content to be edited by any other user;
- they involve the creation of documents (individual pages as well as the entire wiki) without a detailed technical knowledge of HTML;
- they tend towards expressing ideas as relationships between pages, thus creating a network of interrelated topics;

- they are a-temporal, that is, the nodes (or interlinking textual references) change not according to time but by way of development within the evolving and edited text,
- they track the changes to individual pages over time;
- they provide a space where knowledge becomes networked (situated, contextualized) but remains ephemeral: it changes, and can be changed and mediated by the community.

3.5.2 Educational benefits of Wikis

In essence, wikis offer an online space for collaborative authorship and writing. They are available online for all Web users or for members of specific communities, and include version control tools that allow authors to track the history of specific pages, and the history of their personal contributions. Using wikis, students can easily create simple Websites without prior knowledge or skill programming in HTML or current software used for Website authoring, thus eliminating the time overhead necessary to develop these skills. Also, as more organisations adopt the wiki for internal and external collaboration and information, work with wikis at the tertiary level builds crucial skills for the workplace.

A wiki also offers the ability to interact with an evolving document over time. It allows teachers and learners to see the evolution of a written task, and to continually comment on it, rather than offering comments only on the final draft. Considering students' busy schedules, a wiki can also be very useful for tracking and streamlining group projects.

3.5.3 Strategies for using Wikis in teaching and learning

The following are some possible educational uses of a wiki:

- students can use a wiki to develop research projects, with the wiki acting as ongoing documentation of their work;
- a wiki can be used for students to add summaries of their thoughts from the prescribed readings, building a collaborative annotated bibliography;
- in distance learning environments, the tutor can publish course resources like syllabus and handouts, and students can edit and comment on these directly;

- wikis can be used as a knowledge base for teachers, enabling them to share reflections and thoughts regarding teaching practices and allowing for versioning and documentation
- wikis can be used to map concepts: they are useful for brainstorming, and authoring a wiki on a given topic produces a linked network of resources;
- a wiki can be used to facilitate a presentation in place of conventional software, like Keynote and PowerPoint;
- wikis are tools for group authoring of a document;
- wikis are being used for course evaluation: students at Brown University have started CAW (n.d), the Course Advisor Wiki, a place for students to collaboratively write reviews of courses they've taken. CAW gives readers a flexibility to articulate their impressions, and enables richer reviews that combine multiple impressions and perspectives

For a further exploration of some of these ideas, also see *Pearce* (2006), *Wikis in Education and Other Tools for Collaborative Writing* (2006), and *ExamplesWikiUse* (2006).

3.5.4   *Further questions to be explored*

Just as there are strengths in collaborative, co-authored online spaces there are also some challenges. Some wikis have no page locking system, so if two people edit the page simultaneously, one set of changes will be silently deleted. Some wikis do not include a versioning system, making them inappropriate for the task. Also, there are the social issues that occasionally crop up, particularly on very large projects such as the *Wikipedia*. Some pages on *Wikipedia*, dealing with controversial topics such as abortion or religious perspectives, can exhibit a phenomenon known as an "edit war" (Wikipedia, 2006). This is the continuous editing and re-visioning of content by a community member with a particular agenda. The easiest way to circumvent such disagreements is to place a block on the page edit functionality for a period of time.

Asking students to develop new wiki pages can present considerations from an educational perspective which are comparable to teaching students the processes of authorship in any other written task. Depending on the nature of the task at hand, wiki entries may be structurally and procedurally different from standard writing tasks that students may be already used to – therefore, it is important that teachers provide sufficient help and instruction to learners as they come to understand the requirements of the wiki writing genre.

4   Conclusion - An evolving learning ecology

Like the early days of the Internet, there is an optimism driving experimentation and exploration across the learning ecology presented by technology. Web 2.0 presents educators with shifting frames of reference to consider in relation to teaching and learning. Students and educators now have access to a ubiquitous learning environment where it's possible to search for, locate, and quickly access elements of learning that address immediate needs. It is possible to use Web 2.0 technology to construct and organize personalized, unique interactions with an educational context.

The learning design and content elements that form a learning ecology must be dynamic and interdependent. The learning environment should enable instructional elements designed as small, highly relevant content objects to be dynamically reorganized into a variety of pedagogical models. This dynamic reorganization of content into different pedagogical models can create a learning system adaptive to varying student needs. Imagine for example, what could happen if our education curriculum operated more like Web 2.0, YouTube and Wikipedia, allowing for the rapid deployment of scattered expertise and the dynamic reconfiguration of content across contexts. Shifting conceptions of participation and connection for students could be explored and the contrast between "Push" and "Pull" Education (Richardson, 2005) can be mapped across this new learning ecology.

Richardson (2005) suggests that "Push" models indicate students as passive whose needs can be anticipated and shaped by centralized decision-makers. "Pull" models treat students as networked co-creators of media and are designed to accelerate capability building, helping students learn as well as innovate, by pursuing trajectories of learning that are tailored to their specific needs.

In part this shift from "Push" to "Pull" can be seen to relate to George Siemens's (2005) notion of *Connectivism*. Paraphrasing, he indicates that we derive our competence from forming connections.... Unlike constructivism, which states that learners attempt to foster understanding by meaning-making tasks, this theory indicates that the meaning exists and the learner's challenge is to recognize the patterns which appear to be hidden. Meaning-making is seen to involve forming connections between specialized communities and information / knowledge architectures.

Within higher education Jenkins (2007) describes the "YouNiversity" and suggests an intellectual network where students interact not only with professors, but with industry and the community thus encompassing a change in the traditional classroom learning ecology and inclusive of collaborative broader perspectives usually described within a blending of online with face-to-face learning experiences.

Within business the model suggested within 'Wikinomics' (Tapscott and Williams, 2006) indicates that open-source technology and strategies involving mass collaboration "changes everything". That Web 2.0 tools such as wikis can be used successfully to enable tacit and other forms of knowledge to be shared. According to Tapscott, wikinomics is based on four ideas: Openness, Peering, Sharing, and Acting Globally. As educator's considerations of how to translate these ideas into our teaching and learning challenge notions of authorship, intellectual property and "contingency" and "technological imperative" models (Orlikowski, 1992) for the integration of technology to support teaching or learning.

Challenged must be the ways in which our educational system is designed to "push" the limited resources it accessed previously. Explored should be ecologies of access to a plethora of knowledge and resources, and a re-think and expansion of the choices for our students to find those resources most relevant and effective. We need to teach them to take ownership of their own learning and to develop skills in media and information literacy. It is this close examination of Web 2.0 technologies and the discourses that frame their use that attracts the interest of many educators.

Which tools are used by learners and teachers, and whether such tools will be used at all, will always depend on the specific pedagogical needs of a teaching situation. Common to all of these technologies is that they are strongly social and community based. The Blogosphere offers ongoing distributed expression of and interaction with personal news, views, and ideas. Youtube's popularity and authentic slice-of-life offers creative opportunities to share; respond to and author content. Wikis emphasise a more task-oriented collaborative editing of content and development of "collective" interlinked knowledge. The specific focus here on blogs, YouTube and wikis have presented for the reader some initial ideas in order to illustrate and prompt some thought in relation to the use of Web 2.0 technologies.

Such socially-based technologies sit well with the understanding of learning as socially constructed, which has been a cornerstone of recent pedagogical theory. Blogs, YouTube and wikis provide a means to encourage and make visible the social construction of knowledge which such theory postulates, and it is incumbent on teachers to embrace such tools where their use is beneficial to learners and teachers alike.

References

Alexander, B. (2006). Web 2.0: A new wave of innovation for teaching and learning? *Educause Review*, Vol. 41, No. 2., pp. 32-44.

Arreguin, C. (2004) Wikis. In B. Hoffman (Ed.), *Encyclopedia of Educational Technology*. [online], http://coe.sdsu.edu/eet/Articles/wikis/start.htm.

Brown, J.S. (2002) Growing up digital: How the web changes work, education, and the ways people learn. *Journal of the United States Distance Learning Association*, Vol 16, No 2. [online]
http://www.usdla.org/html/journal/FEB02_Issue/article01.html

Course Advisor Wiki. (n.d) *CAW*. [online], http://caw.wikispaces.com/

Clark, R.C. and Mayer, R.E. (2002) *E-Learning and the Science of Instruction: Proven Guidelines for Consumers and Designers of Multimedia Learning*. San Francisco: Jossey-Bass Pfeiffer.

Conway, C. (2006) *YouTube and the Cultural Studies Classroom*. [online], http://www.insidehighered.com/views/2006/11/13/conway

Cunningham, W and Leuf, B (2001): *The Wiki Way. Quick Collaboration on the Web*. Addison-Wesley

Educause Learning Initiative. (2006) *7 things you should know about You-Tube*. [online],
http://www.educause.edu/content.asp?page_id=7495&bhcp=1

ExamplesWikiUse. (2006) [online],
http://www.malts.ed.ac.uk/idel/assignment/wiki/000022.html

Gillmor, D. (2007). *We the Media - 2. The Read-Write Web*. [online],
http://www.oreilly.com/catalog/wemedia/book/ch02.pdf

Godwin-Jones, R. (2007) *Digital Video Update: YouTube, flash, high-definition*. [online], http://www.allbusiness.com/technology/4051526-1.html

Jenkins, H. (2007). From YouTube to YouNiversity. *Chronicle of Higher Education: Chronicle Review*, 53(24), B9–B10.

Lenhard, A., & Madden, M. (2005, November 2). Pew Internet & American Life Project. Reports. Family, friends & community. Teen content creators and consumers. Retrieved December 10th, 2006 fromhttp://www.pewinternet.org/pdfs/PIP_Teens_Content_Creation.pdf

Marzano, R. J. (2006). A Different Kind of Classroom: Teaching with Dimensions of Learning. Retrieved December 4th, 2006 from
http://pdonline.ascd.org/pd_online/
dol02/1992marzano_chapter1.html

Misanchuk, E., Schwier, R., & Boling, E. (1996) Visual design for instructional multimedia. [CD-ROM].

Oblinger, D. (2003) Boomers, Gen-Xers, and Millennials: Understanding the "New Students". EDUCAUSE Review, Vol. 38, No. 4, pp36-40

Olsen, S. (2005) *The 'millennials' usher in a new era*. [online]
http://news.com.com/2009-1025_3-5944666.html

O'Reilly, T. (2005) *What Is Web 2.0, Design Patterns and Business Models for the Next Generation of Software*. [online],
http://www.oreillynet.com/pub/a/oreilly/tim/news/2005/09/30/what-is-web-20.html

Orlikowski, W. J. (1992) The Duality of Technology: Rethinking the Concept of Technology in Organizations. *Organization Science*, Vol. 3, No. 3, Focused Issue: Management of Technology. (Aug., 1992), pp. 398-427.

Paquet, S. (2003) 'Personal knowledge publishing and its uses in research', *Knowledge Board,* [online],
http://www.knowledgeboard.com/cgibin/item.cgi?id=96934&d=744&h=746&f=745.

Pearce, J. (2006) *Using wiki in education. The Science of Spectroscopy.* [online], http://www.scienceofspectroscopy.info/edit/index.php?title=Using_wiki_in_education.

Prensky, M. (2004) *Digital GameBased Learning.* McGraw-Hill, New York.

Richardson, W. (2006) *Blogs, Wikis, Podcasts, and Other Powerful Web Tools for Classrooms.* Thousand Oaks, California: Corwin Press.

Siemens, G. (2005). *Connectivism: A Learning Theory for the Digital Age.* [online], http://www.elearnspace.org/Articles/connectivism.htm

Skiba, D. (2007) *Nursing Education 2.0: YouTube. Nursing Education Perspectives.* Vol 28, No2, pp. 100–102. [online], http://nln.allenpress.com/nlnonline/?request=get-document&issn=15365026&volume=028&issue=02&page=0100#s5

Tapscott, D. (1997) *Growing Up Digital: The Rise of the Net Generation.* McGraw-Hill, New York.

Tapscott, D. and Williams, A. D. (2006) *Wikinomics: How Mass Collaboration Changes Everything.* New York, USA: Penguin Group Publishers.

The ultimate Online Video List. (2007) Retrieved May 20th, 2007 from http://www.everybodygoto.com/2007/05/21/the-ultimate-online-video-list/

Vanderwal, T. (2006). Folksonomy Research Needs Cleaning Up. Retrieved January 23rd, 2006 from http://www.vanderwal.net/random/entrysel.php?blog=1781Wikipedia. (2006) *The edit war.* [online], http://en.wikipedia.org/wiki/Wikipedia:Edit_war.

Wikis in Education and Other Tools for Collaborative Writing. (2006) *Teaching Effectiveness Program*, University of Oregon. [online], http://tep.uoregon.edu/shared/blogswikispodcasts/WikisBiblio.pdf

Microblogging for Reflection: Developing Teaching Knowledge Through Twitter

Noeline Wright
The University of Waikato, Hamilton New Zealand

Editorial Commentary

This paper proposes *Twitter* as a tool for enhancing the self-reflective practices of students concerning learning content and delivery. It differs from the previous chapter as it proposes the use of Web 2.0 tools in classrooms, in real time. As such it is a learning strategy that – like others - erases the frontiers between online and face-to-face learning and may well point to the future of education: from *blurring* frontiers to *disappearing* frontiers.

Wright discusses the latest research in microblogging which involves "learning on the move" or "time shifted learning". Twitter, as an example, gives participants the opportunity to post anything, anytime and anywhere via mobile phones and PDAs and the 140 character limitation requires concise and focused thinking. Wright answers the question, "Does microblogging help teacher education students develop self-reflective practices?" by citing the design of a seven week long integrated course with activities around four reflective topics: retrospection, problem solving, critical reflection and reflection in action. Her conclusions point to microblogging as a modality that boosts community mindedness and a sense of belonging.

Abstract: This paper outlines the use of Twitter, a popular microblogging tool, during student-teachers' experiences of their second secondary school seven-week teaching practicum. The practicum period was a bounded opportunity to trial the efficacy of Twitter as a means by which participant student-teachers could deliberately focus on reflection, by condensing their thinking into 140 character bites. An

71

expected outcome was that regular Twitter use would enhance self-reflective prac-tices about their teaching and the wider practicum experience. Once the practicum ended, participants gathered for a focus group interview to recap the experience and explore the extent to which the intended reflective outcome was achieved. Most of them (out of a cohort of nearly 100) said that the process did indeed en-hance their ability to reflect on classroom experiences in particular, and wider school experiences in general. Having to create posts of 140 characters focused and deepened their thinking about the messages they wanted to convey. The ability to read each other's tweets and respond personally was highly valued, reducing their sense of isolation and, at times, emotional overload. The ability of Twitter to ar-chive ideas and thoughts chronologically provided a rich data set for thematic analysis. The most commonly addressed themes across the expected daily three tweets included: pedagogy, curriculum/lesson planning, relationships (with other staff and students), emotions and classroom management. An unexpected but positive outcome was the desire by some participants to use Twitter the following year. One participant decided that students could use Twitter to not only docu-ment their design-making processes in hard technology classes, but also develop their own reflective practices about these processes. Another has subsequently used Twitter to connect with other subject teachers (Economics) as a means of deepening subject and e-learning expertise.

Keywords: microblogging, Twitter, outcomes, reflection, teacher education

1   Introduction

Microblogging as a Web 2.0 tool is a relatively recent extension of social networking. As a form of expression, microblogging has gained a huge momentum since 2008: Twitter is the most popular version. A 'tweet' (a microblog) is usually posted in answer to the questions like 'What are you doing?' or 'What's happening?' It operates in similar ways to texting (SMS); both tend to limit the number of characters per message. Twitter limits the number of characters to 140 per post. A 'character' is a space, punctuation, numbers and letters.

Early criticism of microblogging argues that tweets are vacuous, spurious and limited. As McFedries (2007) observed, "most people just don't see the point, and others dismiss it as a massive time-suck... [because] of the unremitting triviality of most people's updates". Lyons (2009) argued that Twitter was "a playground for imbeciles, skeevy marketers, D-list celebrity half-wits, and pathetic attention seekers". So, because of such inane, ephemeral microblogging, Twitter's early reviews were not particularly favourable. However, some microbloggers have become highly engaging, garner large numbers of followers, and proliferate links and ideas on a wide range of topics including politics, the arts, technology, social justice issues, and humour. Others have found specific uses related to their work. Lake (2009) and others (Jansen et al. 2009) argue that microblogging is a useful advertising medium for maintaining business presence. Librarians have used it to interact with readers (Kroski 2008), and Jungherr (2008) suggests value in promoting social activism and democratic agendas.

Educationally, a growing network of people use Twitter to share links and ideas, and to communicate with students in courses. Holotescu and Grosseck (2009b), for example, used a Romanian microblogging service in one of their tertiary courses and examined its use among students. They found that students wrote public messages, followed and contributed to discussions, monitored feeds, and, even when the course had ended, continued to collaborate and converse with peers by using this microblogging service. Holotescu and Grosseck considered this latter collaborative and communication outcome was a "very important advantage", alongside the "ambient awareness" of communicating in short posts.

Other researchers have examined Twitter in terms of its topographical and geographical properties (Java, Song, Finin, & Tseng, 2007) and what 'community' might mean within its sphere of influence (Java, Song, Finin, & Tseng, 2009). In terms of a clear focus on learning, both Holotescu and Grosseck, (2009a) and Honeycutt and Herring (2009), examined using microblogging for collaborative learning. For example, Honeycutt and Herring (2009) concentrated on the promotion of deliberate conversational interaction, while Holotescu and Grosseck (2009a) suggested that microblogging was useful for wide range of applications, such as collaborative writing, developing a classroom community, project management, assessing opinion/consensus, being a "platform for metacognition" (p, 73) and being a vehicle for wider, international connections. The ideas in these two studies regarding collaborative learning and metacognition, link closely to this Twitter study.

In other educational research, Aspden and Thorpe (2009) used Twitter to understand the spaces where students learned. Participants posted tweets via mobiles in response to 'Where do you learn?' The authors argued that Twitter gave participants "the ability ... to update anytime, almost any-where, ... through a variety of devices... integral to their lives". Also, the limitations on characters meant that postings were "concise and focused on the key questions". This portability is learning on the move or "time-shifted learning" (Chan and Lee, 2005, cited in Dale & Pymm 2009). Cur-rently, educational microblogging from mobile phones is in its infancy (Wheeler 2009) but is likely to grow.

Wishart (2009) for example, trialled using personal digital assistants (PDAs) with initial teacher education students. Teacher education, Wishart argues, is a programme in which students "are expected to acquire, decipher, and understand a wealth of information, both pedagogical and practical" (p. 266) as they navigate between university courses and the complexities of practicum (school placement) experiences. Wishart's focus on reflection through PDAs plus Aspden and Thorpe's (2009) study using Twitter and mobile phones were the inspirations for this project. What would happen in terms of self-reflection, if teacher education students used Twitter on practicum to comment on their experiences?

2   Teacher reflection

Bengtsson (1995) suggests there are four areas of interest in reflection for educative purposes in teacher education: reflection as self-reflection, re-flection as thinking, reflection as self-understanding and the distancing function of self-reflection. Boody (2008) describes teacher reflection as: (a) retrospection, (b) problem solving, (c) critical reflection, or (d) reflection-in-action. Each of these can map onto the four categories Bengtsson (1995) identifies. 'Retrospection' appears to link closely to self-reflection – the "bending [of] thought backwards to reconsider prior experiences" (Boody 2008, p.498) in order to better understand it and learn from it. In a sense, this also links to Bengtsson's idea of the 'distancing function of self-reflection'. The problem-solving function of reflection has its origins in Dewey's (1933) exploration of reflective thinking in relation to educational processes. It suggests that reflection is a process which helps resolve prob-lems of practice. In this sense it links to reflection as thinking, as does criti-cal reflection (Van Manen 1977; Van Manen 1995). The latter also links to reflection as understanding, and thus the potential distancing function of reflection. Reflection-in-action as a concept and practice derives directly from Schon's (1987) work.

In real terms, developing reflection as a feature of teachers' professional practice is important for a number of reasons. Firstly, it is important because it is a means by which teachers can continue to review and adjust their pedagogical practices for their learners, so their learners have positive learning outcomes. Secondly, it is important for teachers so they can critically examine ideas and practices in a wider educational sense, to judge their value. As Lewis observed, "In a profession as challenging as teaching, honest self-reflection is key. That means that we must regularly examine what has worked and what hasn't in the classroom, despite how painful it can sometimes be to look in the mirror." (Lewis n.d.).Thirdly, these reflective practices and processes are evaluative in a positive way because they suggest openness and a professional on the role of teacher, rather than the role of the personal self particularly when, as teachers, it can be difficult to separate the two. Finally, because "teachers must be able to construct pedagogical practices that have relevance and meaning to students' social and cultural realities" (Howard 2003, p.195), it is important to constantly review how learning opportunities are provided.

3   Study design

This paper therefore reports on a small study examining the value of using Twitter to generate and develop self-reflection during a teaching practicum. Teacher education students were posted to a wide range of secondary schools across New Zealand for seven weeks. The overarching research question guiding this project was "Does microblogging help teacher education students develop self-reflective practices?" The participants, a self-selected group of eight volunteer graduates (approx 9% of the cohort; 4 women and 4 men) in a one-year diploma secondary teacher education course represented diverse subject areas, for example, physical education, music, accounting, Maori language, technology subjects (hard materials and food). During this second practicum, participants were asked to tweet three times each practicum day in response to any of the following questions: What am I learning now?; What do my students say about their learning right now?; What do I need to overcome or solve?; Where am I learning right now?; What am I going to do next?; What is getting in the way right now?; What am I thinking about right now? The tweets became both an individual and collective chronology of reflections and observations spanning seven weeks.

Since Twitter is accessible via mobile phones, it allowed participants to tweet quickly and from anywhere, any time - walking in corridors, during lunch breaks and when passengers in cars on their way home after school each day, or even during classes. However, few used this last option because of schools' policies regarding the use of cellphones at school. Computer-sent tweets, usually posted some time after the fact, were the alternative method of tweeting.

The analysis of both sets of these tweets examined both understandings of the practicum experience, and their deliberate self-reflections, an attribute critical to effective teaching and learning (Beauchamp & Thomas, 2009; Cahill & Adams, 2008; Pollard, 2005; Rich & Hannafin, 2009; Roberts, 2009; Santoro, 2009).

Following the practicum, participants met together on campus to discuss their Twitter experiences. This focus group discussion was digitally recorded as a supplementary data source of themes (content analysis) in relation to both the research question and the tweets. Ideas from all sources were categorised in relation to pedagogy, emotions, relationships, complexity/curriculum/planning, reflections, and other.

4   Findings

Initially, most participants' tweets covered a range of topics, but they soon concentrated on the pedagogy, complexity, curriculum and planning areas. Eventually, they almost exclusively centred on pedagogy. This category, overall, contained the most tweets from all participants. Few tweets addressed the emotional aspect of teaching, but a large number wondered at both the complex and contradictory nature of teaching, and the complex and variable nature of working with teenagers. For example, one participant noted over two tweets, "one student has poor literacy, doesn't want to work and disrupts anyone he can. Teaching includes coming up with a strategy for him…" and, "a teacher cannot control a student's behaviour, but a teacher can manage a student's behaviour". (All quotes are cited verbatim). Another participant observed that she "realised that some kids sit back and pretend they no nothing, but when you give them a task that can be done solo, they strutt it". And when situations became difficult, participants were buoyed by the quickly supportive replies from their peers. For example, one participant was faced with "Heart broken after school by Y12 boy with big personal probs, he was so upset & crying, made me cry! Needs lotsa love & nurturing". The supportive nature of the responses to this participant was one of the key features of mo

As the focus group later revealed, such nimble peer response was highly valued, reducing participants' feelings of isolation and despair. They continued to read each other's tweets, without often responding. Brevity made this easy, and they found comfort reading each other's experiences. Highs and lows were frequently shared. One participant tweeted early in his practicum, "So if 1thing from pract! surely this is to confirm to ourselves that tchng is wat we want 2do! i am convinced it is having a ball!!!!!!!!!!!" and, "So who comes home exhausted but buzzing at the same time?" Holotescu and Grosseck's (2009b; 2009a) studies also valued this sense of ambient community.

Many highs related to relationships with students. For example, one participant said "Y9 [approximately 13 years old] Māori have amazing knowledge retention & are enjoying sharing with the kids who have missed class. Pretty cool...!" Another noted, "hav no cntrol over baggage stds [students] bring 2 class but can redirect or use negativity to good by relationship building. Takes time but happening". Another observed that, "when the lesson reflects your personality, students listen. Students listen to people, not lesson plans or books." He also noted that, "students love boundaries. They know where they stand and what they can do in your class. You just have to set the boundaries."

These tweets directly link to participants' pedagogical experiences in negotiating learning with teenagers, understanding themselves as teachers, and examining the complex nature of teaching. This teacher was beginning to see how important effective relationships were to building a positive learning climate in the classroom. Others were also trying to navigate the collective will of a class to improving and adding to their learning in deliberate ways. For example, "Students just wanted to do practical, no theory. Need to find a balance between what they want and what they need...need to find how to use the practical work to introduce theory concepts." This comment also links to effective student-centred learning practices outlined in Vygotsky's (1978) explanation of the value of the zone of proximal development.

Others acutely observed interactions with their associate teachers and how they worked with students. For example, the physical education (PE) participant noted that she was "cringing inwardly as teacher allows students 2 pick teams 1 by 1 until a cuple are left feeling rejectd and left out". Later, she considered the gender dynamics involved in PE classes in New Zealand, wondering, "R girls 2 intimidated by boys performance? Mayb something 2 b said 4 seperatd PE classes." And later still, tweeted how she had a breakthrough with a student: "stumbled on a way 2 gt a stdnt with behavioural and learnin difficulties 2 do pe 2day. Studnt were recording scores at each diff.. Stations of a circuit. This studnt respnded wel as he is vry methodical and wantd 2 fill out his entire score sheet." This comment indicates her thinking about individual students' learning behaviours, and ways of accommodating them within lessons and indicates something of her developing sense of how to be inclusive to meet diverse learning needs. And since the tweets are archived, she can review the comment later for meta-reflective purposes, linking to Bengtsson's (1995) 'distancing function of self-reflection' and Schon's (1987) reflection-in-action.

By about the middle week of the practicum, the tweets changed from being content- to learner- focus, and gradually concentrated on issues of pedagogy. In the later focus group, participants discussed the extent to which this project helped precipitate deliberate reflection. Without fail, they argued that three tweets each school day forced them to consider not just *what* they did, but *why* and *how*. This eventually meant it was easier to think beyond a lesson's content to its effects and what they could alter. And while it was initially difficult to essentialise thoughts into a tweet, participants felt they thought very deeply about what messages to convey in their few words. In other words, tweeting helped them *know*. This links to the value of reflection as a tool for understanding.

While half of the participants continued tweeting from their mobile phones, the rest reverted to their computers, finding their full keyboard easier to use than their phones' keypads, since most were not qwerty.

However, at least two participants used their mobile almost exclusively, enjoying its portability in capturing their thinking. Perhaps this was an age-related issue. The older participants (these were career-changers in their 40s and older) preferred using their computers to tweet with than the under 30s.

A wider factor was that many felt constrained by their practicum schools' policies regarding cellphone use. Many banned them in classrooms. To mitigate this, those who continued using their phones often waited until break times or after the school day ended. Thus, the intended immediacy of mobiles phones for tweeting reflections was often stymied by constraints beyond participants' control. On the other hand, this delay often suited participants. This greater distance from the event gave them room to rethink before tweeting, and gave them time to compose what each tweet said. So while the sense of the immediate was sometimes lost, later tweets were often deeply reflective. Since all tweets are time-coded, it is easy to see when they were posted. One example, sent after school one day, wondered "re chat in class: what about a deal: work for x minutes in such & such a way, then = x mins for a chat? Possible Win-win?" This reflection suggests that this participant was thinking aloud about strategies to use. Many tweets were also sent in the early morning, before school started, but after these student teachers arrived at school, fitting into the 8.15-8.30am timeslot. These reflected on the day before, as well as thinking aloud about what they wanted to try out or share.

In terms of my role as both researcher and lecturer, it was important to be supportive and at times prick some critical thinking about their thoughts. When one participant mentioned being at home because of illness (swine flu) and feeling upset about missing the first day, it was important to show empathy. When another tweeted a question about students fearing failure in external examinations, I asked, "so what's your thinking about this? how is it affecting kids' learning?" The intention was to provoke deeper thinking.

Tweets failing to fit any of the teaching and learning categories were filed under 'other'. Such posts tended to answer Twitter's 'what are you doing?' question, although participants also shared URLs and responded to each other's more general thoughts. For example, one said, "...Had an ICT lesson well planned that went to custard 2day". They also conveyed information about the wider lives of participants. For example, through this Twitter project, we learned about the health, feeding and sleeping habits of one participant's baby. These greater contextual clues created greater intimacy among participants, and linked to the potential for Twitter to support and sustain learning communities.

The ability to use colloquial and text message conventions meant that tweets reflected not only an idea, but also how the sender felt at the time. Tweets also exhibited turn-taking cues, and punctuation reflected and acknowledged both emotions and social interaction (Borau et al. 2009). One student in particular demonstrated the value of punctuation to convey emotion, when he posted the tweet about "...having a ball!!!!!!!!!!".

In later conversations with some of the participants, they have become excited about the potential to use microblogging with students. For example, one technology teacher sees it as a way of students recording their thinking while developing design project briefs. Another has used it try to connect with similar subject teachers as a way of learning more about teaching in that field. These findings link to Holotescu and Grosseck's (2009a p.78) conclusions about the educative value of microblogging in terms of participants becoming motivated to find their own route, respecting each other and facilitating "mutual awareness [and] responsiveness to the emotions of others" as well a mechanism for posing and sharing problems.

5 Conclusion

This small microblogging project began with the question – "Does microblogging help teacher education students develop self-reflective practices?" Participants used mobile phones and/or computers to send tweets, canvassing thoughts about relationships, pedagogy, planning, curriculum and complexity, plus emotions and reflections on reflections. The 'other' category contained responses and personal tweets revealing aspects of daily life and social interaction: part of how people connect with each other on a regular basis. These participants valued belonging to this Twitter community while on practicum because the regular contact and sense of audience reduced feelings of isolation. And while they initially found that 140-

characters restricted their ability to explain ideas, it soon focused their thinking to reflect purposefully on their experiences. Even though participants were expected to use their mobile phones to transmit their tweets immediately, this was not always possible; half of them used their computers regularly instead. Constraints in schools about their protocols for using mobiles contributed to this, as did the preference for using computer keyboards rather than mobile phone keypads. The study size is a key limitation of the research, but this snapshot may provide the impetus for larger scale or longer term projects focused on eliciting pedagogically reflective behaviours. There is also scope to further examine the role of mentor/teacher, as well as how individual teachers could harness this microblogging tool to support their learners.

What has emerged from this study is that indeed, this microblogging tool supported the development of reflective thinking practices during a school practicum. It also developed a sense of community, reduced feelings of isolation, and created a chronological log of individuals' practicum experiences for subsequent review. The study suggests the potential of such microblogging tools to initiate and sustain learning communities, to be a mechanism for sharing information and questions, and to be a nimble personal support mechanism. It has also excited some participants to use it with their own classes when they begin teaching, and to connect with other subject teachers.

References

Aspden, E.J. & Thorpe, L.P., 2009. Where do you learn?: Tweeting to inform learning space development. Educause Quarterly, 32(1). Available at:
http://www.educause.edu/EDUCAUSE+Quarterly/EDUCAUSEQuarterly MagazineVolum/WhereDoYouLearnTweetingtoInfor/163852.

Beauchamp, C. & Thomas, L., 2009. Understanding teacher identity: an overview of issues in the literature and implications for teacher education. Cambridge Journal of Education, 39(2), 175-189.

Bengtsson, J., 1995. What is Reflection? On reflection in the teaching profession and teacher education. Teachers and Teaching: Theory and Practice, 1(1), 23-32. Available at:
http://www.informaworld.com.ezproxy.waikato.ac.nz/10.1080/135406 0950010103 [Accessed January 18, 2010].

Boody, R., 2008. TEACHER REFLECTION AS TEACHER CHANGE, AND TEACHER CHANGE AS MORAL RESPONSE. Education, 128(3), 498.

Borau, K. et al., 2009. Microblogging for Language Learning: Using Twitter to Train Communicative and Cultural Competence. Available at: http://www.slideshare.net/ullrich/microblogging-for-language-learning-using-twitter-to-train-communicative-and-cultural-competence [Accessed June 20, 2009].

Cahill, B.J. & Adams, E.M., 2008. The couch and the blackboard: adding the 3 Rs of relationships, reactions (emotional), and reflection to the classroom. Journal of Curriculum Studies, 40(5), 671-685. Available at: http://www.informaworld.com/10.1080/00220270802026693 [Accessed September 29, 2008].

Dale, C. & Pymm, J.M., 2009. Podagogy: The iPod as a learning technology. Active Learning in Higher Education, 10(1), 84-96. Available at: http://alh.sagepub.com.ezproxy.waikato.ac.nz/cgi/content/abstract/10/1/84 [Accessed October 31, 2009].

Dewey, J., 1933. How we think: A reassessment of the relation of reflective thinking to the educative process Revised., Boston: D.C. Heath.

Holotescu, C. & Grosseck, G., 2009a. Using Microblogging For Collaborative Learning. In New Technology Platforms for Learning–Revisited. Budapest, Hungary: European Distance and E-Learning Network (EDEN), pp. 71-80.

Holotescu, C. & Grosseck, G., 2009b. Using microblogging in education. Case study: Cirip. ro. In 6th International Conference on e-Learning Applications, Cairo, Egypt (January 2009). Cairo, Egypt.

Honeycutt, C. & Herring, S.C., 2009. Beyond microblogging: Conversation and collaboration via Twitter. In Systems Sciences. Big Island, Hawaii, pp. 1-10.

Howard, T.C., 2003. Culturally Relevant Pedagogy: Ingredients for Critical Teacher Reflection. Theory into Practice, 42(3), 195-202. Available at: http://www.jstor.org.ezproxy.waikato.ac.nz/stable/1477420 [Accessed January 18, 2010].

Jansen, B.J. et al., 2009. Twitter power: Tweets as electronic word of mouth. Journal of the American Society for Information Science and Technology, 60(9), 1–20.

Java, A. et al., 2007. Why we Twitter: Understanding microblogging usage and communities. In Proceedings of the 9th WebKDD and 1st SNA-KDD 2007 workshop on Web mining and social network analysis. San Jose,

California: ACM, pp. 56-65. Available at:
http://portal.acm.org/citation.cfm?id=1348556 [Accessed September 22, 2009].

Java, A. et al., 2009. Why We Twitter: An analysis of a microblogging community. Lecture Notes In Artificial Intelligence, 118–138.

Jungherr, A., 2008. The Digiactive Guide To Twitter For Activism. In University of Seigen, Germany: Creative Commons.

Kroski, E., 2008. All a Twitter: Want to try microblogging?. School Library Journal, 54(7), 31-35.

Lake, N., 2009. Let's Keep It Brief. Smart Computing in Plain English, 20(3), 48.

Lewis, B., The value of self-reflection - any time of year, it's important to self-reflect. About.com: Elementary Education. Available at:
http://k6educators.about.com/od/professionaldevelopment/a/self_refl ection.htm.

Lyons, D., 2009. Don't Tweet on Me. Newsweek, 154(13), 31. Available at:
http://search.ebscohost.com.ezproxy.waikato.ac.nz/login.aspx?direct=t rue&db=aph&AN=44285447&site=ehost-live [Accessed October 17, 2009].

McFedries, P., 2007. Technically speaking: All a-twitter. IEEE Spectrum, 44(10), 84–84.

Pollard, A., 2005. Reflective Teaching: Evidence-informed professional practice 2nd ed., London: Continuum.

Rich, P. & Hannafin, M., 2009. Video Annotation Tools: Technologies to Scaffold, Structure, and Transform Teacher Reflection. Journal of Teacher Education, 60(1), 52-68. Available at:
http://ezproxy.waikato.ac.nz/login?url=http://proquest.umi.com/pqdw eb?did=1652538561&Fmt=7&clientId=8119&RQT=309&VName=PQD.

Roberts, A., 2009. Encouraging reflective practice in periods of professional workplace experience: the development of a conceptual model. Reflective Practice: International and Multidisciplinary Perspectives, 10(5), 633. Available at:
http://www.informaworld.com.ezproxy.waikato.ac.nz/10.1080/146239 40903290703 [Accessed October 27, 2009].

Santoro, N., 2009. Teaching in culturally diverse contexts: what knowledge about 'self' and 'others' do teachers need? Journal of Education for Teaching, 35(1), 33-35.

Schon, D.A., 1987. Educating the Reflective Practitioner: Toward a New Design for Teaching and Learning in the Professions 1st ed., San Francisco: Jossey-Bass.

Van Manen, M., 1977. Linking ways of knowing with ways of being practical. Curriculum Inquiry, 6, 205-228.

Van Manen, M., 1995. On the Epistemology of Reflective Practice. Teachers and Teaching: Theory and Practice, 1(1), 33. Available at: http://www.informaworld.com.ezproxy.waikato.ac.nz/10.1080/135406 0950010104 [Accessed January 24, 2010].

Vygotsky, L.S., 1978. Mind in Society: Development of higher psychological processes M. Cole, ed., Cambridge, USA: Harvard University Press.

Wheeler, S., 2009. Teaching with Twitter. Learning with 'e's. Available at: http://steve-wheeler.blogspot.com/2009/01/teaching-with-twitter.html [Accessed November 1, 2009].

Wishart, J., 2009. Use of mobile technology for teacher training. In Mobile Learning: Transforming the Delivery of Education and Training. Issues in Distance Education. Canada: AU Press, pp. 265-278.

Livechat: Issues of Control

Sue Greener
University of Brighton, UK

Editorial commentary

This paper presents the pedagogical application of yet another Web 2.0 technology: a distant-instant-chat messaging application for the use of students and teachers. Communication is critical in full distance learning but only two channels are possible: synchronous (chat, Skype, videoconferencing …) or asynchronous (emails, discussions boards, walls, forums …). Whatever synchronous tool is used creates a "live" contact between participants and in a full distance learning course, the teacher's presence is crucial. This "live" contact presents the opportunity to check or express understanding, confer expertise, and negotiate meaning, all of which are essential to learning (Lave and Wenger, 1991; Ciussi et al., 2011). Greener argues that best practice involves the creation of thematic chats on organization and timing (for teaching presence), on feelings (for social presence) and on content related topics (for cognitive presence).

Lave, J. and Wenger, E. (1991) *Situated learning: legitimate peripheral participation. Cambridge: Cambridge University Press.*

Charlier B., Ciussi M., Henri F., "Developing innovative practices through collaborative research: recognizing sharing and negotiation of meaning" *ISATT International Study Association on Teacher and Teaching*, 15th BIENNAL "Back to the Future: Legacies, Continuities and Changes in Educational Policy, Practice and Research", Portugal, July 2011.

Abstract: As online learning becomes more widespread in Higher Education (HE), so issues of control become more salient to discussions of learning and teaching. There is widespread recognition that the university teacher's role is increasingly that of facilitator and guide rather than director and total expert (Greener, 2008c, Mentis, 2008), but this raises problems for some teachers as it challenges their pedagogic beliefs, and in turn, can cause them to shy away from interaction in online learning. For these teachers, Virtual Learning Environments can be frightening places in which their expertise is exposed to challenge and students can assume greater power (Greener, 2008a, Greener, 2008b). Even more frightening then, can be the experience of facilitating livechat. Livechat is a synchronous form of Computer Mediated Communication (CMC) which requires all participants to be present online at the same time. In a campus-based course, such communication is likely to serve the purpose of task based groups, or part-time students who have little time for group work or further interaction with their cohort on campus due to the demands of work and family. In a distance education course, livechat can offer perhaps the only directly personal link with remote learners and tutors who may never meet (Greener et al., 2008), unless video conferencing or instant messaging is also enabled. The current emphasis on asynchronous CMC in much online learning may cause problems; according to Haefner (2000), asynchronous communication alone can be "convenient, flexible, inexpensive, less resource-hungry, and, well, lonely?".Livechat has a major advantage for the research practitioner – there is an automatic transcript of the conversation between learners and tutor. These transcripts are immediately valuable in helping all parties recall detail from what can be a turbulent, fast-moving exchange, in order both to reflect and to take action on promises made or problems raised. But for the research practitioner there is an opportunity here, provided ethical guidelines are followed, to explore in detail the process of livechat and dimensions such as turn-taking, social and teacher presence, negotiation of group knowledge, differences of focus and interaction in comparison with face-to-face interaction or asynchronous interaction, as well as the development of critical discourse. According to Park and Bonk (2007), there is still sparse literature on this form of CMC and this may be because it is a daunting experience for many teachers and has thus been taken up far less than its asynchronous cousin. Since it seems likely that the behaviour of the teacher in livechat may have a major effect on any potential learning in this forum (Duemer et al., 2002, Garrison et al., 2003), and that the outcome of critical discourse as well as socialisation is possible and desirable, though not easy (Burnett, 2003, Garrison and Cleveland-Innes, 2005), this study aims to analyse livechat transcripts from an undergraduate course to explore just how control is operated and the impact of control on learning outcomes. WHY OF INTEREST to conference Research practitioners engaged in Higher Education regularly use asynchronous communication tools but not so frequently experiment with synchronous communication (livechat). This study is of direct relevance to those who wish to do so, seeking to understand how teachers and learners relate to issues of control in livechat.

Keywords: chat, synchronous communication, control, pedagogy, eLearning

1 Introduction

As online learning becomes more widespread in Higher Education (HE), not just for distance learning but also for blended delivery where online interaction is used to support and add value to learning opportunities on campus, so issues of control become more salient to discussions of learning and teaching. There is widespread recognition that the university teacher's role is increasingly that of facilitator and guide rather than director and total expert (Greener 2008; Mentis 2008); which is not to deny scholarly endeavour amongst university teachers, but rather to recognise the increasing accessibility of collections of knowledge and information, expertise and teaching materials through the Web. Teachers who have learned their craft before the availability of podcasts, videos and full text scholarly articles, books and other academic resources online, not to mention the opportunities of emailing and videoconferencing with experts around the world, had considerable potential to control the curriculum and the discussion within their classrooms and formed their pedagogic beliefs in this context.

The Web environment can be seen to challenge these beliefs and, in turn, can cause them to shy away from interaction in online learning. For these teachers, Virtual Learning Environments can be frightening places in which their expertise is exposed to challenge and students can assume greater power and control over what is taught, how and when (Greener 2008; Greener 2008).

From this perspective, the experience of facilitating livechat can appear very frightening indeed. Livechat is a synchronous form of Computer Mediated Communication (CMC) which requires all participants to be present online at the same time, but not necessarily in the same place. In a campus-based course, such communication is likely to serve the purpose of task based groups, or part-time students who have little time for group work or further interaction with their cohort on campus due to the demands of work and family. In a distance education course, livechat can offer perhaps the only directly personal link with remote learners and tutors who may never meet (Greener, Greener et al. 2008), unless video conferencing or instant messaging is also enabled.

The sense of exposure of the teacher in livechat and how it affects direction and control of what is to be discussed, and how this should happen, is the subject of this paper. If livechat is seen as important within the design of a course (fully online or campus-based and blended (hybrid)), then it would be worthwhile to look carefully at the issues this produces for the teacher. We might argue that livechat is much less value for learning than asynchronous discussion online, since it ties us down to a time (though not a place) and this seems to contradict the affordances of ICT for learning. However, the current emphasis on asynchronous CMC in much online learning may cause problems; according to Haefner (2000), asynchronous communication alone can be "convenient, flexible, inexpensive, less resource-hungry, and, well, lonely?". Academic conferences on eLearning in Higher Education (HE) abound with perspectives on how to improve engagement in asynchronous discussion. It seems that self-directed learners who are engaged with the subject for whatever reason (for example: assessment, vocation, determination and motivation to learn) are likely to take well to asynchronous discussion for academic purposes. Others will not. Continuing efforts to improve participation in asynchronous discussion (Salmon 2000; Palloff and Pratt 2001; Macdonald 2006; Palloff and Pratt 2007) dating back at least to Gilly Salmon's five step model offer sound guidelines to teachers struggling with this problem, as does recent work by Gabbarre and Gabbarre on training student moderators (2010). Synchronous communication online is the subject of much less research (Park and Bonk 2007).

2 Context of study

Livechat (synchronous communication which is entirely text-based, as for instant messaging, carried out usually within a Virtual Learning Environment) has a major advantage for the research practitioner – there can be an automatic transcript of the conversation between learners and tutor. These transcripts are immediately valuable in helping all parties recall detail from what can be a turbulent, fast-moving exchange, in order both to reflect and to take action on promises made or problems raised. But for the research practitioner there is an opportunity here, provided ethical guidelines are followed, to explore in detail the process of livechat and dimensions such as turn-taking, social and teacher presence, negotiation of group knowledge, differences of focus and interaction in comparison with face-to-face interaction or asynchronous interaction, as well as the development of critical discourse.

In such research analysis, we make the assumption that livechat conversations have a structure which we can study, based on Sachs' constructions of conversation analysis (1992), although when in the middle of livechat, a structure can be hard to spot. The relative scarcity of literature on this form of CMC may be due to lower usage, which in turn may be because it is a daunting experience for many teachers and has thus been taken up far less than its asynchronous cousin. Since it seems likely that the behaviour of the teacher in livechat may have a major effect on any potential learning in this forum (Duemer, Fontenot et al. 2002; Garrison, Anderson et al. 2003), and that the outcome of critical discourse as well as socialisation is possible and desirable, though not easy (Burnett 2003; Garrison and Cleveland-Innes 2005), this study analysed livechat transcripts from a final year fully online undergraduate course to explore just how control is operated and the impact of control on learning outcomes.

The course in question is tutored from the UK but offered to students in a wide range of countries from the Caribbean to South East Asia, including European countries. From the outset, the course design focus has aimed at an online rather than a distance learning experience for students, i.e. students were not simply offered materials with staged assessment submitted and returned with feedback. Learning objects include a weekly video lecture recorded by tutors, online tutorial notes presented in html, not uploaded documents, self-review questions on each week's material, a weekly asynchronous discussion forum in which students present responses to directed tasks and receive timely feedback from tutors, guided references and weblinks and a half-hour livechat session each week in which students can raise problems, ask questions and gain instant response from the tutor. Teaching, in the sense of providing new information and engaging with it, is generally avoided in livechat, which is used primarily as a means to encourage students to learn in a timely way (rather than collecting lecture notes for reading only at end of term revision) and to give tutors the chance to check and develop students' topic understanding and offer clarification of materials. Anecdotal evidence from tutors points to a strong link between engagement in livechat and final assessment grade, though this has not been rigorously analysed to date.

There are of course factors which intervene in the smooth running of live-chat such as server downtimes, poor infrastructure in some countries leading to slow or broken connections, variation between students owning web-connected laptops at home and those who must visit a teaching centre to gain web access with consequent implications for attendance, and of course problematic combinations of time zones across the world. Nonetheless, livechat sessions, originally provided in response to student requests for a more personal touch to teaching online, a way of getting to know tutors and to get answers to problems swiftly, can and do run! When they run, they can present a strange experience for teachers, who are required to mediate communication, technology and culture in one fell swoop. In the process, teachers can easily feel overwhelmed – especially with large groups attending.

3 Conceptual framework

Dialogic interaction is seen by social constructivists as a vital tool in collaborative learning. Discussions of online collaboration have largely picked up this pattern of thinking, and applied it generously to asynchronous and synchronous communication, although there is certainly more research on the former. If we focus on dialogic interaction in face to face learning events, we notice patterns mediated by teachers/facilitators in which some stronger voices naturally dominate, and teachers may or may not make efforts to involve and include weaker voices in the discussion. Of course, not joining in the conversation does not necessarily imply a lack of learning, it simply seems to act as a helpful signal to the teacher that people are engaged in the discussion. When we are dealing with fully online learning events, the text signals of those taking part in conferencing become more important, as a reassurance to the teacher that there are students out there who are engaged. If we cannot see the learners have turned up, we can at least note who logs in and posts online.

If we follow social constructivism thinking, then we see the negotiation of meaning through dialogue as essential to learning. Lave and Wenger's legitimate peripheral participation gives us a way of thinking about the development of that negotiation of meaning, helping us to visualise the journey, or apprenticeship, of the learner from bystander to active and informed collaborator in knowledge construction. Chen et al (2009) suggest that learning happens in a socially situated educational context and this is developed conceptually in the Community of Inquiry model produced by Garrison, Anderson and Archer (2003) which deconstructs the educational experience into overlapping dimensions of social, cognitive and teaching presence.

The literature on synchronous conferencing, with the above ideas on learning, lead us to identify the following difficulties faced by teachers/moderators of livechat:

- Designing the livechat to integrate with and support the course design
- Getting students to participate – face validity, relevance, skills, access
- Facing technology fears in relation to speed and disorder of interaction (unless using a sequenced synchronous communication tool such as Flashmeeting™)
- Providing a comfortable environment in which to develop discussion
- Developing cognitive and metacognitive skills in knowledge construction related to the topic
- Structuring the discussion in livechat, while keeping a focus on the topic

4 Findings

The early analysis of transcripts described in this study looks in particular at point 6 above, in the light of point 3. There is much more to research here, but the initial analysis has focussed on issues of control as seen through the Community of Inquiry model.

Research by Christine McDonald and Birgit Loch applied the Community of Inquiry model to synchronous conferencing in maths teaching (McDonald and Loch 2008). Their coding of indicators of the three types of presence was as follows:

- **Cognitive presence**: Exploration, Confirming no understanding, Confirming understanding, Student repeats, Student propositions, Not commenced work, Question on topic, Integration, Connecting ideas, Resolution and Applying new ideas

- **Social presence**: Affective Apology, Thank you, Emotions, Group cohesion, Social, Greeting, Encouragement, Building community, Organisation Technical (student), Class management (student), Time out (student), Acknowledge receipt, Nodding
- **Teaching presence**: Design and organisation, Time out, Technical, Course management, Class management, Facilitating discourse, Clarification, Focused question, Giving task, Confirming under-standing, Steering in direction, Direct instruction Explanation of content, additional explanation/definition

Accordingly, this livechat transcript analysis has used these descriptions to look for signs of cognitive, social and teaching presence in 18 transcripts taken from 3 different cohorts (2008, 2009 and 2010) of students studying a Research Methods course online (final year undergraduate). Numbers of students attending these livechat sessions, which are optional and not as-sessed, vary from thirty to two. Sessions were sampled across the duration of the 12 week course, with six samples from each cohort. Although some researchers favour a more holistic analysis approach, Garrison et al (2006) suggest that such transcript analysis is invaluable in understanding pat-terns of interaction.

Cognitive presence: In all transcripts there was evidence of cognitive presence as students asked questions about their understanding of weekly topics. Questions on cognitive understanding were usually thickly inter-spersed with process understanding concerning assessment, navigation of module site, technical infrastructure, literature sources etc. In terms of CoI therefore, students were demonstrating cognitive presence but at the same time in consecutive postings could flip into social or teaching pres-ence.

Social presence: Naturally there was more social interaction at start and end of sessions, as for a face to face encounter. However students were comfortable exchanging social comments throughout sessions, including encouragement to others, advice on process or technical issues, and apologies where they felt they had not achieved what they were supposed to do. Nodding was frequent as some students show they are engaged and signal presence without contributing a substantive posting. There was much more social presence than would normally be the case in a face to face discussion in class, as students connect across different centres and, like the tutor, need the reassurance of continued personal connection in what may seem an impersonal environment. Although body language cannot be seen, students were on the whole adept using emoticons and social abbreviations used in text language (LOL etc) which kept the dialogue rich and connected.

Teaching presence: this was demonstrated by students almost as much as by the tutor in the majority of transcripts in terms of course management, focussed questions, steering in direction and adding additional explanation. Certain elements such as initial explanations, facilitating discourse, giving tasks and direct instruction were inevitably associated mainly with the tutor.

Transcript review showed that the tutor was not wholly "in control" of how the discussion proceeded, despite repeated efforts to ensure topic questions were addressed, it was fairly easy for students to steer the discussions towards their own preoccupations. Given the nature of livechat discussion, this is not a bad thing. In order for students to gain a role in the learning community of the module, it is essential that they establish a strong presence and in livechat this can be done readily by taking a role in leading questions. Online there is less overt signalling of teacher "power" (no position in "front" of the class for example), which allows students to take over this role. In some cases this is a chance to compete for attention, as in a face to face class, but it is usually easier for a student to make their presence felt online (than to do this in a physical class) simply by posting: no need to compete for the teacher's attention, this is automatically given by the medium in a way which looks equal in status to the teacher's interventions.

One disadvantage evident in the transcripts was timing. In this course, livechats were confined to middle of week sessions because Friday is not possible for many students in Muslim cultures. This meant that students had usually had insufficient time to read all the weekly materials before livechat, with the result that cognitive discussion and outcomes were less emphasised than the tutor might have wished. On reflection, however, this made the discussions more personal and supportive than didactic – a useful outcome when livechat is just one element of the learning design, there were other ways (asynchronous task-focussed discussion and tutorial materials etc) to focus on cognitive outcomes.

5   Conclusions

The focus of this initial analysis of transcripts was to look at how discussions were structured to focus on topics and review how easy or difficult it was for the tutor to keep control of the discussion. Conversation analysis assumes an orderliness about conversation which can be studied. There was little orderliness demonstrated in these transcripts, particularly in sessions where there were more than five students attending. The hectic and overlapping nature of these discussions in real time means the tutor must concentrate on ensuring questions do not go unanswered and endeavour to build a sense of logic out of an apparent morass of diverse comments and questions on process of learning, assessment, infrastructure, timing, navigation and learning design as well as substantive topic discussion.

Burnett's study showed it was feasible for synchronous CMC to "address social, organisational and intellectual aspects of discussion through online chat (Burnett 2003 p298) and this was certainly confirmed by this initial analysis. Others argue that while social presence alone will not ensure the development of critical discourse, it is difficult for such discourse to develop without it (Garrison and Cleveland-Innes 2005). This was evident in the transcripts where social comment was often the "glue" constructing the narrative and enabling students to engage in the session, even when their own questions could take some time to be answered.

Where there were more than ten students attending the session, there was a clear diminution of the teacher's role in demonstrating teacher presence, with this being taken over on many occasions by students who guided others, answering their queries and summarising problems. While the teacher's role was pivotal in most cases in setting the tone of the discussion and building the framework for discussion, it was the students who led discussion and ensured their concerns were the main focus. For example sessions where the teacher attempted to stay focussed on the key weekly materials in the VLE were often dominated and subverted by students' emphasis on assessment concerns, rather than learning concerns.

This suggests that a livechat, although apparently an inherently chaotic interaction, may have a consistent role in supporting the students' overriding concerns. Rather than being an overt teaching medium where knowledge about the subject is the focus, it is the co-construction of knowledge about online learning which takes centre stage. Attempts by teachers to "control" the session, as would be common in a physical face to face environment, towards the achievement of planned learning outcomes may be fruitless if students are more concerned with other aspects of their current learning activity. As a forum for the achievement of learning unplanned by the teacher but central to the needs of the student, livechat may be a particularly effective tool.

References

Burnett, C. (2003). "Learning to chat: tutor participation in synchronous online chat." Teaching in Higher Education **8**: 247-261.

Chen, Y., N.-S. Chen, et al. (2009). "The use of online synchronous discussion for web-based professional development for teachers." Computers and Education **53**: 1155-1166.

Duemer, L., D. Fontenot, et al. (2002). "The Use of Online Synchronous Discussion Groups to Enhance Community Formation and Professional Identity Development." The Journal of Interactive Online Learning 1(2).

Gabarre, C. and S. Gabarre (2010). Virtual Communities of Knowledge: Assessing Peer Online Moderators' Contributions. Fifth International Conference on ELearning (ICEL), Penang, Malaysia, Academic Publishing Ltd.

Garrison, D. R., T. Anderson, et al. (2003) "Critical Inquiry in a text-based environment: computer conferencing in Higher Education." The Internet and Higher Education **Volume**, 87-105 DOI:

Garrison, D. R. and M. Cleveland-Innes (2005). "Facilitating Cognitive Presence in Online Learning: Interaction is Not Enough." American Journal of Distance Education **19**(3): 133.

Greener, A. R., S. L. Greener, et al. (2008). Strategic Learners at a Distance. 3rd International Conference on ELearning (ICEL08) Cape Town, SA, Academic Conferences Ltd.

Greener, S. L. (2008). Exploring Readiness for Online Learning, University of Brighton, School of Education.

Greener, S. L. (2008). Identity crisis: who is teaching whom online? European Conference on ELearning (ECEL) 2009. Agia Napa, Cyprus.

Greener, S. L. (2008) "Self-aware and Self-directed: Student Conceptions of Blended Learning." Merlot Journal of Online Learning and Teaching **Volume**, DOI:

Haefner, J. (2000). "Opinion: The Importance of Being Synchronous." Retrieved 30/04/2010, 2010, from http://wac.colostate.edu/aw/teaching/haefner2000.htm.

Macdonald, J. (2006). Blended learning and online tutoring. Hampshire, UK, Gower.

McDonald, C. and B. Loch (2008). Adjusting the community of inquiry approach to a synchronous mathematical context. ASCILITE. Melbourne.

Mentis, M. (2008). "Navigating the eLearning Terrain: Aligning Technology, Pedagogy and Context." The Electronic Journal of eLearning **6**(3): 217-226.

Palloff, R. M. and K. Pratt (2001). Lessons from the Cyberspace Classroom: the Realities of Online Teaching. San Francisco, Jossey-Bass.

Palloff, R. M. and K. Pratt (2007). Building Online Learning Communities. San Francisco, Jossey-Bass.

Park, Y. J. and C. J. Bonk (2007). "Synchronous learning experiences: Distance and residential learners' perspectives in a blended graduate course." Journal of Interactive Online Learning **6**(3): 245-264.

Sachs, H. (1992). Lectures on conversation. Oxford, Basil Blackwell.

Salmon, G. (2000). E-moderating: The Key to Teaching and Learning Online. London, Kogan Page.

Students and Blogging: How to Map the Informal Learning Process?

Monika Andergassen, David Moore, Andrea Gorra and Reinhold Behringer
Leeds Metropolitan University, Leeds, UK

Editorial commentary

This paper offers another point of view on distance learning: it investigates learning in informal contexts, outside traditional course settings. The authors study informal blogging among students with the challenge of understanding that *informal learning* is "...not institutional, not planned, and not structured" (p. 20). This type of learning results from life's daily activities related to work, family or leisure contexts where learning may not be intentional, but occurs nonetheless. In their research the authors identified such learning in terms of transversal competencies, including cognitive skills (writing, synthesis) and socio-affective domains (comments producing feelings of frustration or self satisfaction). Cardon, Fouetillou and Roth (2011), who study the blogosphere, argue that without comments blogs are destined to disappear. Blogs also raise important questions about self-branding and digital identity (Warburton, 2010), concepts which need to be addressed by students in a formal learning context since mastering these skills is necessary in professional life.

Cardon, Dominique; Fouetillou, Guilhem; and Roth, Camille. (2011). "Two Paths of Glory - Structural Positions and Trajectories of Websites Within their Topical Territory." ICWSM 5th AAAI International Conference on Weblogs and Social Media. Barcelona, Spain.

Warburton, Steven. (ed.) 2010. *Digital Identity Matters*. London: King's College London http://www.rhizomeproject.org

Abstract: With the increasing focus on lifelong learning due to the fast changing labour market, informal learning is gaining growing attention. In the research about learning, the potential of Web 2.0 technologies, such as weblogs, wikis, or social networks, has been described extensively in recent years. Some of the strengths are seen as arising from their bottom-up development, having emerged in the living contexts of the internet users, and from their active nature, making the users active producers of content instead of just passive consumers. Many projects have adopted weblogs, wikis, or combinations of them, in formal learning contexts, and have drawn connections to learning theories, such as constructivist learning. However, few studies have investigated the learning processes triggered by the new applications, in particular when they are used outside of course settings, in informal learning contexts. The study presented in this paper aimed at empirically investigating these learning processes, by researching the case of informal blogging by students. Semi-structured interviews were held with 6 students of the Vienna University of Technology as part of a larger empirical study investigating the participation, the motivations and the learning processes of blogging students. The interviews were analysed on the basis of the model of experiential learning developed by Lloyd Davies. Davies' model describes learning as a multidimensional process which includes, among other parameters, expectations, emotions, previous experiences, reflections and insights. The results of the interview analysis show that all students went through learning cycles in the course of their blogging. The learning cycles were initiated for instance by social experiences, such as unexpected feedback of people on weblog entries, or absence of comments in the weblogs. The interview analysis indicates that the informal use of weblogs triggers various learning processes. It can be concluded that weblogs might serve as learning tools outside of institutional curricula, and that they support informal learning.

Keywords: Weblog, higher education, web 2.0 and learning, informal learning, learning process, learning assessment, multidimensional learning

1 Introduction

The current paper aims at increasing the understanding of possible connections between blogging in informal contexts and learning. It builds upon two trends which have been discussed extensively in the educational sciences in the last years: informal learning and web 2.0. According to Straka (2004), informal learning and non-formal learning have been gaining increasing attention in recent years, together with an increasing attention towards lifelong learning. As Rohs (2007) argues, the latter is caused by the societal and technological changes in the knowledge society. The European commission, as a proponent of lifelong learning, defines it as "all learning activity undertaken throughout life, with the aim of improving knowledge, skills and competences within a personal, civic, social and/or employment-related perspective" (European Commission 2001, p.9). The European Commission proposes distinctions between formal, non-formal and informal learning, as presented in Table 1.

Table 1: Definition of formal, non-formal and informal learning (Source: European Commission 2001)

Formal Learning	Non-Formal Learning	Informal Learning
Learning typically provided by an education or training institution, structured (in terms of learning objectives, learning time or learning support) and leading to certification. Formal learning is intentional from the learner's perspective.	Learning that is not provided by an education or training institution and typically does not lead to certification. It is, however, structured (in terms of learning objectives, learning time or learning support). Non-formal learning is intentional from the learner's perspective.	Learning resulting from daily life activities related to work, family or leisure. It is not structured (in terms of learning objectives, learning time or learning support) and typically does not lead to certification. Informal learning may be intentional but in most cases it is non-intentional (or "incidental"/ random).

Similar to the definition of informal learning by the European Commission, Marsick and Watkins (1990, p.12) argue that informal learning is strongly related to incidental learning, being "a by-product of some other activity, such as task accomplishment, interpersonal interaction, sensing the organisational culture, trial-and-error experimentation, or even formal learning". Some researchers, like Colley et al. (2003), question the distinction between non-formal and informal learning, on the grounds that the strict separation of the categories does not help to understand the meanings, purposes and contexts of learning. However, although informal learning is not defined consistently throughout the literature, three basic conditions are consistently mentioned, according to Rohs (2007, p.28), namely that informal learning is not institutional, not planned, and not structured.

As with informal learning, web 2.0 and its associated technologies and tools have been discussed broadly in educational research in the last few years. The term 'web 2.0' is used to describe a compound of concepts, projects and practices (Alexander 2006), including the shift from a 'Read Web' to a 'Read-Write Web' (Downes 2005), where the users contribute and exchange data and content collectively (O'Reilly 2005).

One of the web publishing formats associated with the web 2.0 is weblogs. Weblogs are diary-like websites, consisting of entries sorted in inverse chronological order, where every entry is date stamped and provided with a unique URL, and commentable by other users. The potentials of weblogs for education are seen, among others, in their learner-centeredness (Baumgartner et al. 2004), their support in the construction of knowledge (Du & Wagner 2005) and in the enhancement of reflective competency (Brahm 2007).

2   Weblogs and learning in the literature

In a literature review covering the years 2007 to March 2010, undertaken among 13 journals, among those 7 commercial and 6 open access journals, and the ERIC scientific database, 21 scientific articles were found which describe empirical studies concerning learning with weblogs.

The studies were situated in various seminar settings, such as health care, language training or education. The results concerning learning gains were generally positive and included cognitive, motivational, social and emotional learning aspects.

For instance, findings regarding the cognitive dimension included an enhancement in the organising of information of the students through the use of weblogs (Tekinarslan 2008) and the development of writing skills (Bloch 2007; Makri & Kynigos 2007; Tekinarslan 2008). While some researchers found positive connections between blogging and the enhancement of reflective competency (Murray & Hourigan 2008; Ladyshewsky & Gardner 2008), other studies reported indications of non-critical writing of students (Farmer et al. 2008; Leslie & Murphy 2008).

The social aspects of blogging in educational contexts included the increase of peer interaction through blogging (Oomen-Early & Burke 2007; Leslie & Murphy 2008; Churchill 2009; Y. Huang et al. 2009), a positive influence of discussions in the weblogs on the projects of the course (Fessakis et al.

2008), and the development of inter-cultural competencies (Elola & Oskoz 2008).

All the studies investigated weblogs that were being used in the context of a formal course. Indeed, in most set ups, weblogs were part of the course assignments. None of the articles describes blogging outside of seminars. Just 3 articles (Armstrong & Retterer 2008; Kerawalla et al. 2009; Leslie & Murphy 2008) describe projects where blogging was not marked. However, weblogs were a course requirement or would enhance the overall course mark in these articles.

Thus, the current study aims at making a contribution to the research about blogging and learning by investigating blogging outside of course settings, with no formal requirements and no assessment pressure connected to it.

3   Do students learn when blogging in informal contexts?

Studying this question raises a number of methodological difficulties. First, when blogging in informal contexts, students might not blog with the intention to learn. Indeed, few students report that they use weblogs for learning (Ebner et al. 2008), and reported motivations to start blogging concern issues other than learning (Andergassen et al. 2009). A second difficulty is that, in contrast to weblogs in seminar settings, in an informal context it is difficult to compare students' skills 'before blogging' and 'after blogging'. Reinmann (2005, p.43) defines learning as a change of one's own perceptual structure, which might lead to a change in one's own behaviour, thinking or perception. In an informal context it is not known in advance whether a student will start a weblog, at which specific time he will start it, and for how long he will blog. Establishing cause and effect relationships becomes extremely problematic, therefore.

Given this, the current study seeks to elicit, via interview, the perceptions of the students about their experiences with blogging. The aim is, by decomposing the abstract concept of learning, to be able to trace possible learning processes that occur during the process of blogging, even if the students themselves would not recognise them as learning processes.

Specifically, the following research questions are addressed:

- Can the learning processes of the students be mapped to a model of learning?
- What, if anything, do the students learn?

The study was undertaken at the Vienna University of Technology, Austria (TU Vienna). A free weblog service for all students and staff members has been offered by the TU Vienna since 2004. The weblog service allows every member of the university to open one or several weblog accounts. The weblogs can be used in courses, but also outside of seminar settings, on a voluntary basis and without grading, where everybody is free to choose the themes for their own weblog. The current study refers to these as 'informal usage scenarios'.

4   Davies' model of experiential learning

The empirical study was based on the model of experiential learning proposed by Davies (2008), presented in Figure 1. Davies adopts Kolb's definition of experiential learning, where "Learning is the process whereby knowledge is created through the transformation of experience" (Kolb 1985, p.38).

The core item in Davies' model as the starting point of learning is experience, represented in the centre of Figure 1. An experience is, according to Davies, always active and personal in nature, varying in time span, and varying in complexity. In this multidimensional model, a variety of elements interacts with the experience, and plays a role in how an experience is processed further, potentially leading to learning. Davies (2008, p.19) argues that these elements come into play "as we convert experience into lessons, concepts, or generalized ways of behaving which we can use in the future".

The elements are marked with the letters A through to N in Figure 1.The elements A through to D, namely expectations (A), emotions (B), opportunity (C) and learning orientation and memory (D), describe the personal premises for the way an experience is perceived and processed. The elements E through to J, namely own observations (E), fellow participants' observations (F), informed non-participant observations (G), formal knowledge (H) and own experience (J), represent possible sources of information which might be addressed in the process of learning. Finally, the elements K through to N, namely reflection (K), insight (L), credibility checking (M) and the experience bank (N), describe the steps in the process of learning.

Davies uses a cloud-like shape of the elements to represent his notion that they are not fixed in nature, but rather subject to interpretation and change. The only exception to this representation is 'reflection and insight'. This is shaped like a prism, to illustrate the notion that, similar to the separation of light through a prism, the reflection and insight phase in a learning process enables the learner to understand the complex components involved with an experience. The arrows in Figure 1 indicate that the elements are interconnected and that iterations among them might occur in the process of learning.

This model was chosen because it approaches learning as a multi-dimensional process, and because the model's emphasis on real-life experiences as the basis for learning, was seen as making it applicable to informal learning contexts, following the definition given in Table1.

5 Empirical study: Qualitative interview analysis

5.1 Data collection

Six semi-structured, one-hour interviews were held with students of the TU Vienna. The students selected for the interviews were active bloggers who had been authoring a weblog at the TU Vienna for at least 6 months at the time of the interviews. The interviews aimed at eliciting the perceptions of the students about possible connections between their blogging and learning, following the model of experiential learning discussed in section 4.

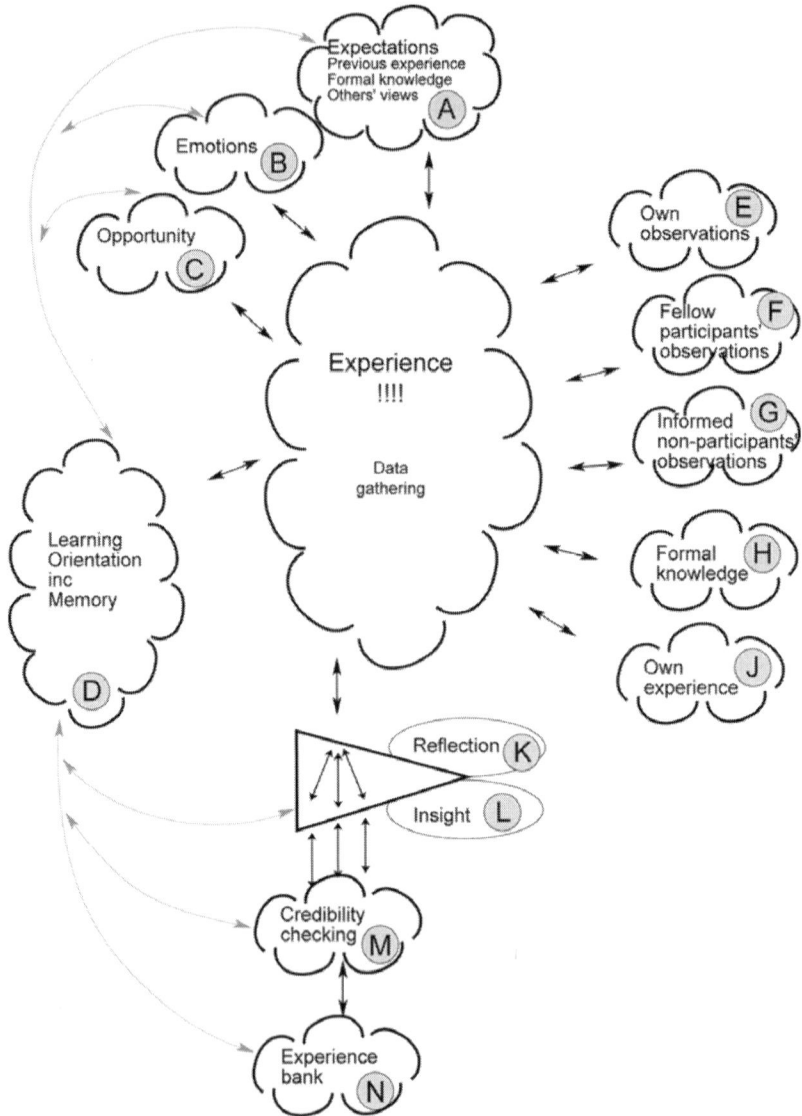

Figure 1: Model of experiential Learning (Source: Davies 2008)

Davies suggests a set of reflective open questions to ask oneself when exploring one's own learning in the light of the elements of his model, including, for instance, questions such as "What exactly were your experiences with ... ?", or "What emotions did you feel at the start of the experience, and how did the emotions change as the experience unfolded?". Davies' questions were adopted for the semi-structured interviews.

The students were encouraged to reflect on their blogging, to think about the influences of, for instance, emotions and previous experiences on the current experience, and to reflect about insights gained through blogging and the application of these insights in new contexts.

5.2   Data analysis

The analysis of the interviews considered both Lamnek's (2005) description of four general steps in the analysis of qualitative interviews, and Creswell & Clark's (2006) procedures in qualitative data analysis. The following five steps were applied:

(Step 1) Transcription and preparation of data:
As a first step, the interview audio files were transcribed and anonymised, including the changing of the names of the interviewees.

(Step 2) Exploration of data:
To gain an overview of the interview data, all the interviews were read through, notes were made in the transcripts about emerging ideas or patterns, and a short summary was written about each interview. An example of the short summary of interview #1 is presented in Table 2. A codebook was developed for the detailed analysis of the interviews, based on the elements of Davies' model.

Table 2: Summary of interview with Bob (above), and citation from the interview (below)

Summary
Bob started his weblog about a year ago. He blogs about everything that affects his personal life, several times a week. From the beginning, he has been receiving comments to his posts, and notes that as a positive experience. Besides the weblog, he writes for various media and has attended a workshop on writing. Bob notes that his blogging has moved from a spontaneous action to a planned activity throughout the year, outlined in the citation below:

Citation	
„Es hat sich auf jeden Fall verändert, weil ich es jetzt nicht mehr spontan mache, sondern in gewisser Weise strukturiert, also schon zumindest alle paar Tage gern einen Eintrag habe, beziehungsweise schon bewusst schaue, was kann ich schreiben, was will ich schreiben. Das hat sich definitiv verändert, also das ist jetzt nicht so, dass ich spontan irgendwas mache, sondern das ist schon geplant" (Bob, lines 869-879, original German transcript)	*"It has definitely changed, because I don't do it [blogging] spontaneously any more, but in a certain way structured, so I want to have an entry at least every few days, and accordingly I think consciously about what I can write, what I want to write. This has definitely changed, it is not that I do something spontaneously, but it is planned."* *(Bob, translation to English by authors)*

(Step 3) Individual analysis:

In the analysis of the individual interviews, the coding of the interviews was done. Passages deemed not relevant were dropped, leading to a reduction of the interview material, and relevant passages were grouped according to the codes. Table 3 presents an example of a coded passage of the interview with Bob.

Table 3: Coding of passage of interview with Bob

Citation and Code		
„ich freue mich eigentlich über jeden Kommentar, der irgendwie verursacht wird."	*"I am happy about every comment I get"*	Emotion: is happy when people write comments
(Bob, lines 123-124, original German transcript)	*(Bob, translation to English by authors)*	(Code)

To visualise the coded sections of the interviews, and the relationships among them, maps were produced in the style of Davies' model of experiential learning. An example is presented in Figure 2.

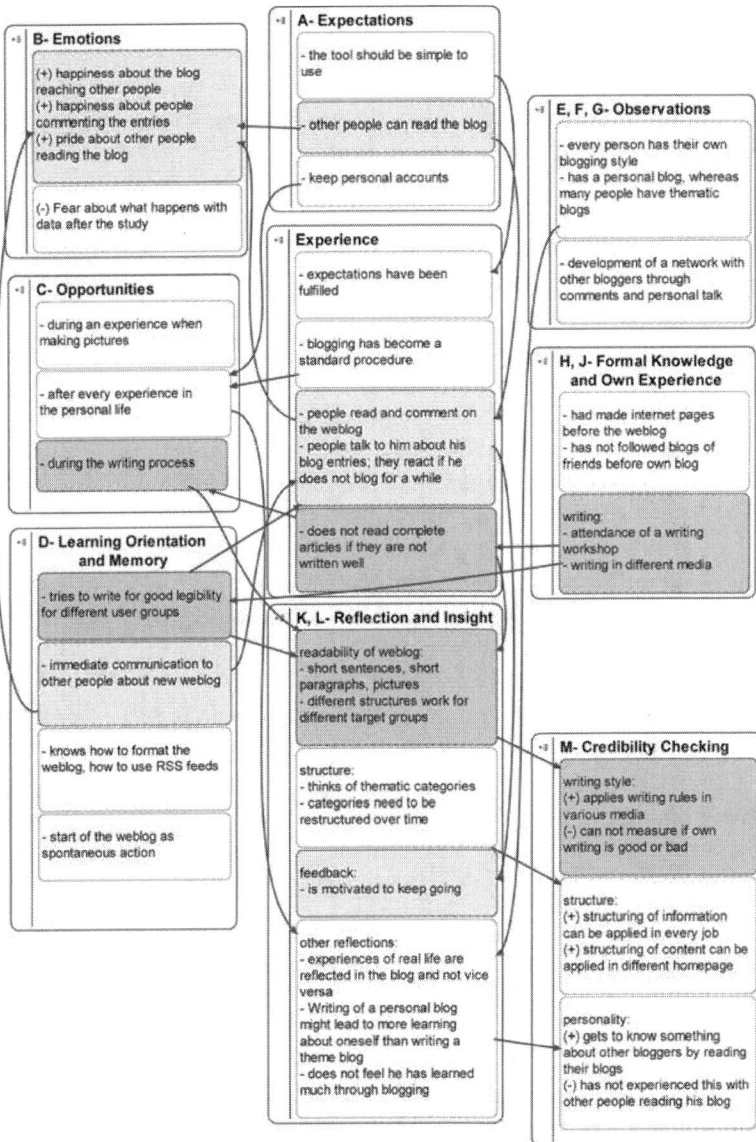

Figure 2: Visualisation of the interview with Bob according to Davies' (2008) model of experiential learning

In a similar manner to Davies' model, the experiences are at the centre of the map. It can be seen that a variety of experiences were had by Bob, for instance that "blogging has become a standard procedure" or that "people read and comment on the weblog". The arrows among the elements indicate their dependencies. For instance, Bob's *experience* that "people read and comment on the weblog" was preceded by the *expectation* that "other people can read the blog", and followed by the *emotion* of "happiness about the blog reaching other people". Interconnected elements are coloured in light grey and dark grey, respectively, for a better overview.

(Step 4) Generalised analysis:
After analysing the individual interviews, commonalities and differences among the interviews were investigated, and emerging themes were generalised where appropriate. Table 4 presents an example of the comparison about how the interviewees tried to adapt to their readership:

- Marc has adapted his writing towards providing the information that the readership was expecting from him, instead of writing about his originally intended themes.
- Simon sees the weblog as a one-directional communication tool, and does not care about comments.
- Jeff has stopped trying to copy the writing style of other people, since he did not get any comments, and started to write about things that derive from him personally.

Table 4: Comparison of interview passages about how the comments (or lack of them) by other people would influence one's own writing

Citations	
„ich habe dann die Informationen geliefert, die die anderen haben wollten (…) Und nicht das, was ich eigentlich ursprünglich vielleicht über den Blog transportieren wollte."	*"then I have provided the information which the others wanted to have (…) And not what I wanted to transport through the blog originally."*
(Marc, lines 939-945, original German transcript)	*(Marc, translation to English by authors)*

"Für mich ist der Blog ein ein-direktionales Kommunikationsding (…) Früher hatte jeder seine Homepage und hat dort irgendwelche Sachen geschrieben, heute hat er einen Blog."	"For me, the blog is a one-directional communication tool (…) In the past, everybody had their homepage and has written things in there, nowadays they have a blog."
(Simon, lines 847-852, original German transcript)	(Simon, translation to English by authors)
„Angefangen habe ich so mit, quasi so fast ein bisschen, teilweise ein bisschen kopiert, ehm wie andere Leute bloggen (…) Aber ich bin eher dazu übergegangen, dass ich eben fast nur Sachen blogge, (…) die ich gemacht habe, die von mir stammen, oder irgendwelche Ideen von mir zu bloggen, und weniger so ein News-Relay zu sein, also das hat sich ein bisschen geändert"	"I have started with, I almost a little bit copied how other people blog (…) But I have migrated to just blog about things (…) which I have done myself, my ideas, and less to be a news relay, well this has changed a bit."
(Jeff, lines 33-44, original German transcript)	(Jeff, translation to English by authors)

(Step 5) Control phase:
Throughout the analysis process, the original transcripts were consulted to avoid misinterpretations or the omission of important themes in the process of reducing and grouping.

6 Results and discussion

The analysis of the interviews indicates that students go through various learning processes when blogging in informal contexts. Referring to the research questions, the following findings were made:

6.1 Can the learning processes of the students be mapped to a model of learning, and how?

The schedule of questions for the qualitative interviews was based on Davies' model of experiential learning. In the analysis process of the interviews, the coded fragments of the interviews were visualised according to the model. As is shown in Figure 2 for the interview with Bob, the accounts of the students could be grouped according to Davies' elements, and various connections among the elements were found, indicating learning processes taking place. Thus, learning processes of students could be mapped with the model of experiential learning by Davies. The following example describes one of these learning processes:

6.1.1   *Comments and feedback*
Bob's *expectation* before starting the weblog was that other people could read his weblog. He then had the *experience* that people, even strangers, would read and comment on his entries. People talked to him about his weblog and reacted if he did not blog for a while. The feedback caused positive *emotions* in Bob. He was happy and proud that his weblog would reach other people and that they would comment on his writing. As an *insight* he notes that the positive feedback motivated him to keep blogging.

6.2   What, if anything, do the students learn?
Among other themes, two aspects emerged in all the interviews, namely comments and feedback as a social dimension of learning, and the development of the writing style as a cognitive dimension.

6.2.1   *Comments and feedback*
Most students reported about their *experience* of getting comments or feedback by other people. This would cause positive *emotions*, like pride that people read the weblog, surprise that people reacted on the weblog, and joy. However, Tom reports about emotions like frustration if his articles would not cause any comments. Marc reports about having received many comments on stories of conjoint events with his friends, but few comments on "deep" stories, like personal accounts of political events or similar. Jeff reports about not getting any comments at all, which caused frustration in the beginning.

The reflections and insights from these experiences and emotions vary among the students, and thus different learning processes are triggered by the experiences and emotions. Marc, for instance, was responsive to what readers wanted and focused on writing about conjoint events, and less about what he wanted to transport through the weblog originally. Jeff, by contrast, would focus on his personal interests and his direct output, and not try to assimilate any more, after not getting any comments anyway.

6.2.2 Development of the writing style

All 6 students emphasise the importance of the writing style for a weblog, and five students report to have improved or adopted their writing style during their blogging:

When reading articles of other weblogs, Bob has had the *experience* that he does not read the whole articles if they are not written well. To improve his writing, he had thus attended a writing workshop before the start of his weblog and brought this *formal knowledge* into blogging. He creates *opportunities* to reflect about his writing every time he writes an entry, and according to his *learning orientation* he aims at writing for good legibility. He gains the *insight* that short sentences, short paragraphs and the inclusion of pictures increase the readability of a weblog. Also, he notes that different structures work for different user groups. He applies the learned writing rules in various media and thus *checks their credibility*. However, he can not measure if his own writing is good or bad.

By comparison, Tom adopts a casual style of writing, Marc builds up the stories following the structure of including an opener, a few pictures, a picture description, and some joke. Simon orients his writing style towards particular book authors he likes. Andrew learned that an article should not be too long or too short, and that structuring the article with bullet points would help the readers who just quickly drop by.

Overall, then, our data suggests that blogging in informal contexts triggers learning processes regarding personal writing style, and regarding the feedback of other people.

7 Conclusion

The current paper aimed at investigating possible links between blogging in informal contexts and learning. The model of experiential learning by Davies was applied to the development and analysis of qualitative interviews with students. The results indicate that (1) Davies' model supports the mapping of informal learning processes by breaking them down into elements, and that (2) blogging in informal contexts triggers various learning processes, for instance regarding the adaptation of the individual author's writing style or the reaction on comments and feedback.

It should be noted that the study has some limitations. The number of the interviewees was relatively small in this study. A larger number of interview partners would be helpful to support and further extend the findings. Furthermore, all the interviewees were students at university level. The results are thus applicable only to this user group. Also, it should be noted that all the interview partners were male students, as no female students reacted to the invitation to take part in the interviews.

Another possible limitation lies in the research method. The coding of the qualitative interviews is subject to possible bias. Some measures were taken against this bias, including the constant comparison of the codes among the interviews to assure a similar coding from the first to the last interview, and the consultation of a second coder for a part of the interviews.

Finally, to get more robust insights into the suitability of Davies' (2008) model of experiential learning for describing the learning processes of students, the interviews should also be analysed along other models of learning. Further research would be needed to deepen the understanding about whether the elements proposed by Davies suffice to describe learning from experience.

Despite these limitations, the results of the study give valuable evidence to indicate that weblogs might serve as learning tools outside of institutional curricula, and support informal learning.

References

Alexander, B. (2006) Web 2.0: A New Wave of Innovation for Teaching and Learning? Educause Review, 41(2), 32-44.

Andergassen, M., Behringer, R., Finlay, J., Gorra, A., Moore, D. (2009) Weblogs in Higher Education - Why do Students (not) Blog? Electronic Journal of e-Learning, 7(3), 203-215.

Armstrong, K. & Retterer, O. (2008) Blogging as L2 Writing: A Case Study. AACE Journal, 16(3), 233-251.

Atteslander, P. (2008) Methoden der empirischen Sozialforschung 12th ed., Schmidt (Erich), Berlin.

Baumgartner, P., Bergner, I. & Pullich, L. (2004) Weblogs in Education - A Means for Organisational Change. In Multimedia Applications in Education (MApEC) Proceedings. Multimedia Applications in Education. Graz, pp. 155-166.

Bloch, J. (2007) Abdullah's Blogging: A Generation 1.5 Student Enters the Blogosphere. Language Learning & Technology, 11(2), 128-141.

Brahm, T. (2007) Blogs - Technische Grundlagen und Einsatzszenarien an Hochschulen. In "Ne(x)t Generation Learning": Wikis, Blogs, Mediacasts & Co. - Social Software und Personal Broadcasting auf der Spur. Themenreihe 1 zur Workshop-Serie. St. Gallen.

Churchill, D. (2009) Educational applications of Web 2.0: Using blogs to support teaching and learning. British Journal of Educational Technology, 40(1), 179-183.

Colley, H., Hodkinson, P. & Malcom, J. (2003) Informality and formality in learning: a report for the Learning and Skills Research Centre, Leeds: University of Leeds. Available at: http://www.hrm.strath.ac.uk/teaching/postgrad/classes/full-time-41939/documents/formalandinformallearning.pdf [Accessed January 12, 2009].

Creswell, J.W. & Clark, V.L.P. (2006) Designing and Conducting Mixed Methods Research, Sage Pubn Inc.

Davies, L. (2008) Informal Learning: A New Model for Making Sense of Experience, Gower Publishing Ltd.

Downes, S. (2005) E-learning 2.0. eLearn Magazine. Available at: http://www.elearnmag.org/subpage.cfm?section=articles&article=29-1 [Accessed August 25, 2008].

Du, H.S. & Wagner, C. (2005) Learning with Weblogs: An Empirical Investigation. In System Sciences, 2005. Proceedings of the 38th Annual Hawaii International Conference on System Sciences. HICSS'05. pp. 7b-7b.

Ebner, M., Schiefner, M. & Nagler, W. (2008) Has the Net Generation Arrived at the University? - oder Studierende von Heute, Digital Natives? In Offener Bildungsraum Hochschule. Freiheiten und Notwendigkeiten. Medien in der Wissenschaft. Münster: Waxmann.

Elola, I. & Oskoz, A. (2008) Blogging: Fostering Intercultural Competence Development in Foreign Language and Study Abroad Contexts. Foreign Language Annals, 41(3), 454-477.

European Commission (2001) Communication from the Commission. Making a European Area of Lifelong Learning a Reality, European Commission. Available at: http://www.bologna-berlin2003.de/pdf/MitteilungEng.pdf [Accessed February 4, 2009].

Farmer, B., Yue, A. & Brooks, C. (2008) Using blogging for higher order learning in large cohort university teaching: A case study. Australasian Journal of Educational Technology, 24(2), 123-136.

Fessakis, G., Tatsis, K. & Dimitracopoulou, A. (2008) Supporting "Learning by Design" Activities Using Group Blogs. Educational Technology & Society, 11(4), 199-212.

Huang, Y., Jeng, Y. & Huang, T. (2009) An Educational Mobile Blogging System for Supporting Collaborative Learning. Educational Technology & Society, 12(2), 163-175.

Kerawalla, L. et al. (2009) An empirically grounded framework to guide blogging in higher education. Journal of Computer Assisted Learning, 25(1), 31-42.

Kolb, D.A. (1985) Experiential Learning: Experience as the Source of Learning and Development, Prentice Hall International.

Ladyshewsky, R. & Gardner, P. (2008) Peer assisted learning and blogging: A strategy to promote reflective practice during clinical fieldwork. Australasian Journal of Educational Technology, 24(3), 241-257.

Lamnek, S. (2005) Qualitative Sozialforschung: Lehrbuch 4th ed., Beltz Psychologie Verlags Union.

Leslie, P. & Murphy, E. (2008) Post-Secondary Students' Purposes for Blogging. International Review of Research in Open and Distance Learning, 9(3).

Makri, K. & Kynigos, C. (2007) The Role of Blogs In Studying The Discourse And Social Practices of

Mathematics Teachers. Educational Technology & Society, 10(1), 73-84.

Marsick, V.J. & Watkins, K.E. (1990) Informal and Incidental Learning in the Workplace, Routledge.

Murray, L. & Hourigan, T. (2008) Blogs for specific purposes:

Expressivist or socio-cognitivist approach? ReCALL, 20(1), 82-97.

Oomen-Early, J. & Burke, S. (2007) Entering the Blogosphere: Blogs as Teaching and Learning Tools in Health Education. International Electronic Journal of Health Education, 10, 186-96.

O'Reilly, T. (2005) What Is Web 2.0. Design Patterns and Business Models for the Next Generation of Software. Available at: http://www.oreillynet.com/lpt/a/6228 [Accessed April 17, 2008].

Reinmann, G. (2005) Blended Learning in der Lehrerbildung 1st ed., Dustri.

Rohs, M. (2007) Zur Theorie formellen und informellen Lernens in der IT-Weiterbildung. Universität der Bundeswehr Hamburg. Available at: http://opus.unibw-hamburg.de/opus/volltexte/2007/1230/pdf/2007_rohs.pdf [Accessed February 5, 2009].

Straka, G.A. (2004) Informal learning: genealogy, concepts, antagonism and questions, Bremen: Unstitut Technik und Bildung, Universität Bremen. Available at: http://www.itb.uni-bre-men.de/downloads/Publikationen/Forschungsberichte/fb_15_04.pdf [Accessed March 7, 2009].

Tekinarslan, E. (2008) Blogs: A qualitative investigation into an instructor and undergraduate students' experiences. Australasian Journal of Educational Technology, 24(4), 402-412.

Web 2.0 Practices for Peer Assessment Processes: Exploring the Synergies and Tensions

Geraldine Jones
University of Bath, UK

Editorial commentary

The introduction of peer assessment processes into a formal learning environment may be facilitated by Web 2.0 practices. Geraldine Jones explores this hypothesis in this chapter, together with the notions that Web 2.0 practices value user-generated content, are designed to incite user participation, promote cultural openness, and incite crowd-sourced feedback that may be worth as much or more than that of an expert. But the formal learning context raises some issues, such as institutional frictions where peer review might be seen as the transfer of an important responsibility to a learner's population. This is also a strong argument for the introduction of peer review when addressing large populations, however, as it liberates professorial time. Another similar issue involves the risk of obtaining unreliable assessments because learners may lack the necessary confidence or skills. Jones discusses these matters, grounding her reflection on a case study based on the use of Voicethread – a collaborative tool allowing oral discussion about digital content. Her findings are quite surprising: Web 2.0 practices were not completely endorsed by the two learner populations in this context, and yet collaboration and peer assessment appeared successful.

Abstract: The participatory practices (Jenkins 2006) surrounding web 2.0 services at first sight appear attractive to harness for the purposes of peer assessment (Falchikov 2007). But specifically what practices act as enablers for effective feedback (Nicol & MacFarlane-Dick 2006) and what tensions occur when web 2.0 practices for peer assessment are introduced into formal teaching and learning settings? This paper seeks to shed light on these questions through presenting, analysing and discussing the findings from a small scale participatory study in which two cohorts (n=18,n=15) of first year undergraduate students created, peer reviewed and assessed each others' digital story (McDrury & Alterio 2003) productions using the Voicethread web 2.0 service (http://voicethread.com). A key component of this innovative assessment practice (now in its second year) is the central role of the student, specifically in negotiating appropriate assessment criteria. A critical evaluation of data from student surveys, focus groups and comments left as peer feedback will be used to discuss insights into: The impact on the student experience of adopting web 2.0 practices for assessing their peers. The extent to which the affordances of the web 2.0 service enabled or constrained the assessment. In the light of the findings from this study the paper will conclude by exploring the usefulness of the concepts outlined in the 'big ideas' (Anderson 2007) in guiding the adoption of web 2.0 practices for peer assessment and whether any reinterpretation is helpful when deploying web 2.0 services for assessment in formal academic contexts.

Keywords: peer assessment, feedback, web 2.0, Voicethread, digital story

1   Introduction

In a climate where we are encouraged to exploit new technologies for learning there is notable rhetoric surrounding how contemporary learners' use of web 2.0 services in support of informal learning activities will transform existing formal teaching and learning practices (Elliot 2007, Downes 2007). The potential benefits of harnessing the creative, collaborative and communicative activities associated with web 2.0 services for learning in academic contexts have been outlined and widely discussed (Walker et al. 2010, McLoughlin & Lee 2007, Burden & Atkinson 2008). However the extent and ways in which learners engage with web 2.0 tools and services can be diverse and some would argue rather more modest than rhetoric suggests (Selwyn 2008). Furthermore there is little empirical evidence as yet, of transformation of current teaching and learning practice driven by learners' informal use of web 2.0 services. Reasoning that our educational institutions (schools, universities) are unlikely in the near future, to change radically, Selwyn (2008) encourages us to focus on investigating how to integrate web 2.0 services into existing teaching and learning contexts. Peer assessment is one area where arguably, there are potential synergies between the assessment practices institutions seek to foster and the participatory, informal learning cultures that draw on and invite comment and critique by others. While the benefits of involving peers in assessment are well known (Falchikov 2007), designing, developing and managing effective peer assessment processes can present challenges, for example a large investment of tutor time. Some studies investigate the use of technology to improve the efficiency of peer assessment processes (Davies 2008) but few explore how peer assessment processes can be supported through contemporary networked technologies and associated participatory cultures. This paper seeks to illuminate, through a case study analysis, the extent to which a web 2.0 service can be harnessed to the enterprise of undergraduate peer feedback and assessment. An assessment process in which first year students created, shared and critiqued digital story productions via the Voicethread web 2.0 service forms the case under scrutiny here.

To set this study in context this paper begins by reviewing the benefits and challenges of peer assessment as outlined in the literature before moving on to explore the synergies apparent between peer assessment processes and participatory web 2.0 cultures. Following this the case is presented and analysed in detail thereby exposing this innovation for its intrinsic value (Stake 2000). To conclude the case is revisited discussed for its instrumental value (Stake 2000), drawing out lessons learned about peer assessment in a web 2.0 world.

2 The benefits and challenges of peer assessment in higher education

Before proceeding further it is useful to define what is meant by peer assessment and indicate the rationales underpinning its use. According to Falchikov (2007)

> *"Peer assessment requires students to provide either feedback or grades (or both) to their peers on a product, process or performance, base on criteria of excellence for that product or event which students may have been involved in determining." (p132)*

Implicit in this definition is a shift of power towards learners taking on more responsibility for tasks that previously were solely the domain of their tutors.

There may be both learner and teacher centric motivations for introducing peer assessment; for example it could be underpinned by a desire to develop core educational skills necessary for life long learning or to save tutor time particularly where large teaching groups are involved. Ideally benefits for both learners and tutors would be sought, however if the dominant motivation is teacher centric then it may prove difficult for the tutor relinquish power and successfully devolve some of the responsibility for assessment to the students (Boud 1994).

The benefits of peer assessment for learners have been well documented (see for example Falchikov 2005) and include improved critical thinking and communication skills, cognitive and metacognitive competency, self confidence and personal development. In addition students in receipt of feedback from their peers are likely to use it to inform judgements about their own work, so peer assessment activities may be viewed as a means of developing self- assessment skills. Seemingly learners are not the only potential beneficiaries, some tutors implementing peer assessment processes have reported increased professional satisfaction and enhancement of their own assessment practice (Falchikov 2007).

Typically concerns associated with peer assessment surround the issues of reliability and validity (Falchikov 2007). Students who lack confidence can question their own or their peers competency in awarding marks and some find it challenging to ensure the judgements they are making on others' work is fair.

3   Web 2.0 and peer assessment

Of the six characteristics or 'big ideas' associated with Web 2.0 as described by Anderson (2007), four may be considered of particular relevance to peer assessment practices.

User generated content: Web services such as Flickr , YouTube and many others invite users to generate content by providing a quick and easy way of publishing it. Individuals can show case (for free) their digital creations for viewing by the general public or to a more select group of 'friends'. In these services there is a built in means for making available digital assessment products to a group of peers for the purpose of receiving feedback.

The power of the crowd: The idea here is that large groups of knowledge-able individuals are said to be able to make better decisions than individual experts; wikipedia being a case in point. Crucially web 2.0 services provide the means for collecting and aggregating opinion and knowledge from many individuals so arguably there is potential for students to gain valu-able feedback from large numbers of their peers which may turn out to be equally or more valuable than that received from a single tutor.

Architecture of participation: This refers to the many ways in which web 2.0 services invite participation, notably by providing the facility for users to 'talk back' or build on content produced by others. Most blogs and wikis invite comment and services or digital artefacts can be combined or 'mashed-up' to generate new content. Collecting feedback from peers could occur simply by making use of the 'talk back' utilities of web 2.0 ser-vices.

Openness: Web 2.0 is said to be characterised by an underlying philosophy of openness. This is not only manifest in the use of open source software but also by the willingness of web 2.0 participants to freely share informa-tion and resources with each other under creative commons which offers a more permissive approach than copyright to the attribution of sources.

This last 'big idea' moves us away from the functionality of web 2.0 tech-nologies and their technical suitability for supporting peer assessment ac-tivity and onto issues related to the dispositions of those engaged in web 2.0 activities. Jenkins (2006) coined the phrase 'participatory cultures' to describes these dispositions. According to Jenkins (2006) a participatory culture is one;

> *"With relatively low barriers to artistic expression and civil engage-ment*
>
> *With strong support for creating and sharing one's own creations with others*
>
> *With some type of informal mentorship whereby what is known by the most experienced is   passed along to novices.*

Where members believe their contributions matter.

- Where members feel some degree of social connection with one another"(p7)

  Arguably trying to foster the participatory cultures that have grown up around web 2.0 services for peer assessment could help facilitate key enablers of the process, namely empowering students and engendering a more student centred approach. However there may be potential challenges associated with taking this approach in traditional HE contexts, for example;

- Not all students may be familiar with informal participation in web 2.0 activity (Lenhardt and Madden 2005), so equity of access and skills development could be an issue.
- The dominant assessment culture experienced by students in HE, that of externally imposed targets, rewards and retribution, may run counter to the participatory cultures linked to a web 2.0 experience.
- What motivates participation in informal web 2.0 activity may differ from what motivates students to participate in peer assessment processes using a web 2.0 platform. The later may prove less compelling than the former.
- The expectations and dispositions of participation and involvement evident in informal social web 2.0 contexts may not easily transfer to web 2.0 contexts engineered for peer assessment activity.

The extent to which these benefits and challenges are manifest and whether or not Web 2.0 approaches amplify or diminish the strengths and weaknesses observed in traditional implementations of peer assessment are of interest when considering the case study presented here.

4   Case Study - Voicethread and peer assessment

4.1   Context

This case focuses on a peer assessment activity introduced on a first year undergraduate unit, 'Exploring Effective Learning', which forms part of an undergraduate degree in Coach Education and Sports Development (CESD) at the University of Bath. The aims of the unit are to identify effective approaches to learning, and develop student understanding of the learning process in the context of study in (Higher Education) HE. A key aspect of this unit is to develop student ability to reflect on and critique their own personal approaches to learning. The unit is well established and has always been assessed by a 3,000 word assignment however students studying this unit are new to the university and unfamiliar with assessment practice in HE. A broader concern is that students embarking on this degree programme are assessed primarily through written texts (12 assignments and 9 examination questions) judged solely by their tutors. This provides little variety for the students and tutors and fails to develop digital literacy that is increasingly a feature of contemporary working life.

4.2 Aims and objectives

Broadly the aim of this study was to change and diversify assessment practices on this first year unit to more effectively support student learning. More specifically the objectives were:

- To introduce a new mode/product of assessment that complements rather than replaces the tutor marked written essay assignment.
- To develop student critical thinking skills through the introduction of processes that involve peers in making judgements about the quality of each others' work.
- To promote a student centred approach to assessment by fostering a participatory culture akin to those that exist around web 2.0 services
- To raise student awareness of the purposes of assessment in HE and the learning opportunities it provides.

4.3 Implementation

A digital story assignment was introduced to where students were asked to produce a creative, reflective analysis of personal insights into their own effective learning. This was presented as an audio-visual production using still images with a scripted commentary. These digital story productions accounted for 24% of the total mark for the unit.

Students from two cohorts (n=18, n=15) participated in the development of an individually focussed digital story. Cycles of feedback from their peers and their tutors (Table 1) supported students in developing their stories.

The responsibility of summatively assessing the digitals stories was shared between peers and tutors. Thus in total students contributed 12% of the marks awarded to their peers.

Table 1: Activities scaffolding the development of individual digital stories *(after McDrury and Alterio 2003)* showing feedback/assessment responsibility

Phase	Activity	Feedback responsibility
1	Telling & Listening & Questioning Dialogue	Peers
2*	Developing assessment criteria Dialogue	Peers and tutors
3	Drafting (text) & Analysing Formative feedback	Peers and tutors
4	Scripting, image selection Formative feedback	Peers and tutors
5	Drafting media production Formative feedback	Peers
6	Final Production Summative Assessment Event	Peers and tutors

* introduced for the second cohort of students only.

Students used the Voicethread web 2.0 service (http://voicethread.com) to author their stories and exchange formative feedback. Voicethread presents a highly intuitive user interface that arguably supported even those with little or no previous multimedia skills in creating multimedia productions by following three easy steps (Figure 1).

Figure 1: The Voicethread user interface

4.4 Summary of findings

Student surveys (n=17) and focus groups conducted with each of the co-horts at the end of the unit contributed data to the findings about the impact of this peer assessment activity on the student experience. Personal reflections captured the tutor's perspective.

4.4.1 Student participation

After receiving feedback from tutors and peers most students responded by refining their digital stories. However in the early phases of story development feedback from tutors was more in evidence while in the final phases peer feedback was more prevalent (Figure 2).

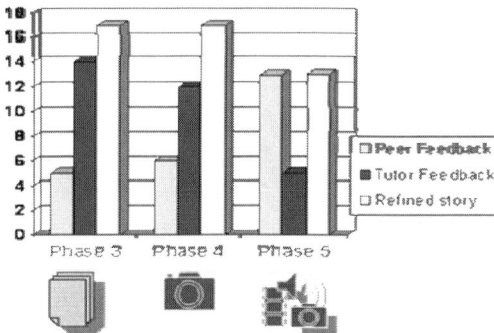

Figure 2: Students who received feedback from peers and tutors and refined their stories at intermediate phases of development. (cohort 1)

125

4.4.2 The role of peers

Furthermore the survey data showed that feedback from tutors and peers seemed to complement each other. For example the majority of students were prompted to make changes to their stories as a result of tutor feedback but half of all students relied on examples of peer work to help them decide whether or not their own stories are improving (figure 3 & 4).

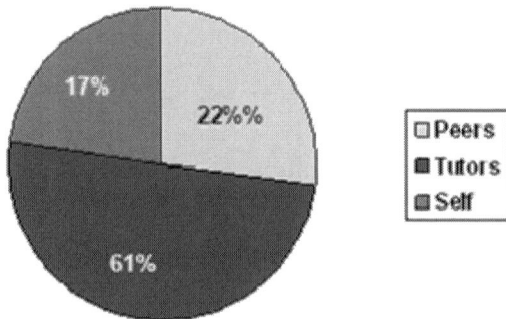

Figure 3: Percentage of students who were influenced to refine their stories by feedback from their tutor, peers

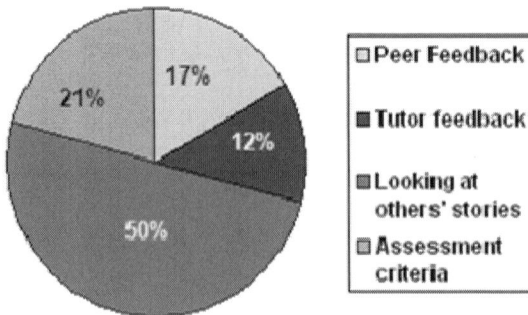

Figure 4: Percentage of students drawing on different sources of information to decided whether or not their stories were improving

Giving feedback to others helped inform students' judgements about their own stories as exemplified by these comments from students:

> *"Giving feedback helped us in a way because we could compare ours to theirs." (F3)*

> *"When I was comparing my story with another persons I could see whether I had more or less content and whether theirs was more of a story and they'd drawn conclusions." (M4)*

However there were indications that social pressures were inhibiting some students in being honest with their feedback for example:

> *"Yes , it was hard to be putting constructive criticism that isn't going to feel like damning to them" (M2)*

> *"It was difficult to give a criticism. I found I just gave positive, like saying 'This is good, this is good'. I didn't necessarily go 'Actually, if I were you I'd change this' because you felt a bit weird doing that." (M1)*

4.4.3 *Motivation*
Some students commented in positive ways on the novelty and more personal nature of the digital story assignment. The students who commented as follows clearly found the task enjoyable.

> *"It's nice using something different to just an assignment. I think you learnt more doing it that way as well."*

> *"It's not like just going to the library, finding a book, getting a reference, it's just a bit different"*

> *"More of a personal attachment as well because it's your personal experience"*

4.4.4   Taking on the role of assessor

Judging by student opinion as sampled in an end of unit survey overall students felt able and comfortable to adopt their new role. For example from cohort 1 (n=17):

- 59% - thought it was appropriate to contribute to summative assessment of their peers
- 88% - felt able to contribute to the final assessment of peers work
- 71% - felt comfortable with contributing to the final assessment of peers work
- 76% - thought the assessment criteria adequately supported them in making decisions about their peers work.

4.4.5   Reliability of peer judgements

When the marks awarded by students to their peers were compared to those awarded by the tutors there is a notable discrepancy (Figure 5). One likely reason for this discrepancy might be that undergraduate students are less experienced in marking work than their tutors. It should also be noted that the students themselves expressed doubts about the reliability of their peers judgement. However there may be other factors at play such as differing interpretations put on the meaning of the assessment criteria.

4.4.6   Students developing assessment criteria

All members of the focus group thought that their involvement in developing the assessment criteria was a worthwhile activity, principally because it helped them to better understand the nature of the assignment product that they were creating.

"you knew where you were heading"

"it helped you produce it yourself because you knew roughly what was required"

"it's not crafting your story for being a story. It's more crafting it for what the criteria say."

Students found their own discussions around the assessment criteria most useful in developing their understanding of the digital story assignment. Applying the criteria then helped further.

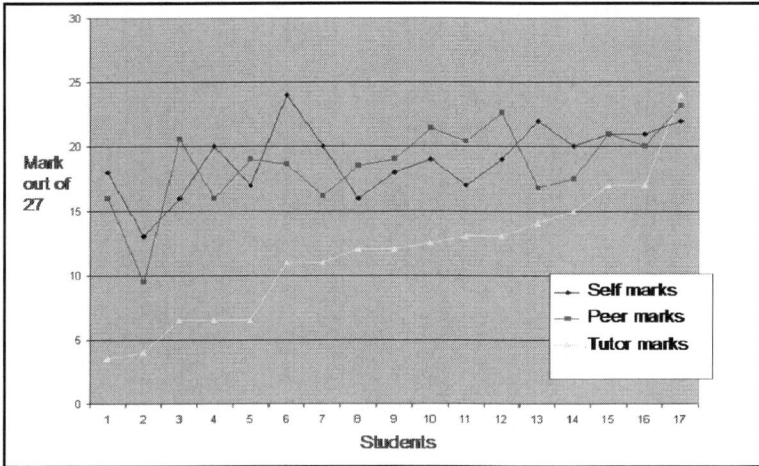

Figure 5: A graph comparing average marks awarded by tutors (n=2), peers (n=9) and a speculative self awarded mark for each student in cohort 1

Despite having considerable involvement in developing the assessment criteria student could see room for improvement after having used them in earnest. When it came to the summative assessment event there was a great deal of concern about marking another student's work as fail.

> *"If you are friends with someone you don't want to give them a fail but sometimes you kind of should"*

4.4.7 Did involvement in developing criteria make for better peer assessors?

In cohort 2 there were fewer low marks, peer and tutor marks were better aligned but peer marks were still generally higher (figure 6). As with cohort 1, students' self assessments showed little correlation with either peer or tutor marks.

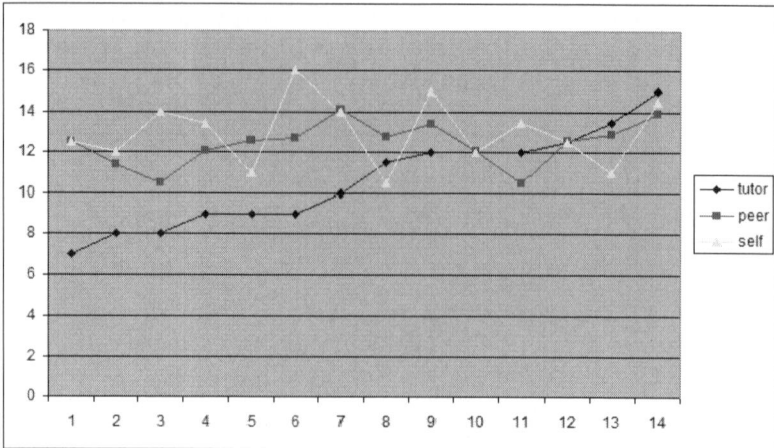

Figure 6: A graph comparing average marks awarded by tutors (n=2), peers (n=7) and a speculative warded mark for each student in cohort 2

As a result of this investigation into a web 2.0 enabled peer assessment process around a digital story production, a number of benefits and challenges for the students and tutors emerged.

4.5 Benefits

- Both the students and the tutor noted that digital story was a welcome diversification from the usual written pieces of coursework. Tutors also commented that the digital story products proved efficient to mark in terms of time.
- The Voicethread service proved to be particularly valuable in giving access to others' work in progress, thus sparking self assessment activity.
- The task of developing assessment criteria engendering a sense of collective ownership of the nature of the product and the process through which it was developed. The concentrated work on the development of the criteria also ensured that students formed a clear idea of what would be assessed. This increased student awareness of assessment processes in HE in general, and problematised assessment criteria (their function, value, issues such as weighting, bias towards content/presentation etc) in particular.

- The summative peer assessment event seemed to empower students who took their task extremely seriously, many taking the opportunity to provide their peers with additional optional written comments as well as the mandatory numeric score.
- Students studying this unit began to see assessment as an activity that helped shape their final assessment products, and one in which many had input, their peers, tutors and themselves.

4.6 Challenges

- The (well documented) problem with peer assessment of how to deal with bias was also evident in this case study. Students reported feeling less inclined to award low marks to their peers. This was managed to an extent by keeping the level of peer contribution to final marks at a low level but substantial enough to ensure that students saw it as worthwhile.
- Issues of reliability were voiced by the students and tutors. However familiarisation with the criteria through involvement in their development helped, to an extent, to improve the reliability of peer judgement.
- The quality of the formative peer feedback was low lacked criticality even though students were supported in formulating constructive formative feedback. As mentioned previously social pressures may have proved inhibiting.
- The design and management of the peer assessment process was time consuming for the tutor. Cycles of formative feedback beginning in face to face group work and later moving to the Voicethread service had to be planned and scheduled. It was only in the latter stages of the process that students felt empowered to take this on themselves.
- The digital story productions were unfamiliar assessment products for both students and tutors. Locating the digital story genre in the overall scheme of assessment was problematic at first and it took time to discover what was these digital products were particularly good at assessing in the specific context in question.

5 Discussion

Overall, what can we take from this case study with respect to the contribution made by the Voicethread web 2.0 services to peer assessment activity?

Voicethread has been broadly characterised as a discourse facilitation web 2.0 service (Mejias 2005). It allows asynchronous commenting around a multimedia artefact, where comments may be text or audio, input from a variety of devices (e.g. computer, mobile phone). Voicethread was not specifically designed with teaching and learning in mind however its pedagogic potential has been analysed in detail (Burden & Atkinson 2008), but it remains largely unexploited in authentic learning contexts. The pedagogic analysis carried out by Burden and Atkins, takes a somewhat deterministic approach, using technological affordances as a starting point to map out how Voicethread could be used to create a number of possible and arguably highly idealised student centric learning environments. This and similar approaches, I would argue, can prejudice our assumptions about the nature learning environments supported by web 2.0 services. Namely, that interactions are spontaneously collaborative, privileging the expertise of the learners and diminishing the role of the tutor. Following this thinking we might have expected the peer assessment activity mediated by Voicethread presented in this case study, to be driven by rich student-student conversations featuring high quality, high volume critical comment centred around individual digital media productions. However critical discourse was not a prominent feature of the learning environment under scrutiny.

The key contribution of the Voicethread service was in providing a platform for vicariously learning from the examples of digital stories made available by and for peers. Students noted that viewing the stories of others was instrumental, over and above the formative feedback provided by peers, in helping them decide whether or not their own stories were improving. Access to others' work stimulated self-assessment through enabling comparisons of quality. This is a well documented and valuable bi-product of peer assessment processes. Student initiated sharing of digital stories stimulated peer feedback which was often reciprocated thus a sense of mutual support and responsibility to others was perpetuated. Even though the feedback left by peers lacked criticality and was typically non-directive it may still have been making a significant contribution to the peer assessment process (Cho & McArthur 2010).

An important enabler for participation in the peer assessment activity was the control that Voicethread afforded each individual account holder who determined when and with whom to share their digital productions. Arguably this and the fact that tutors did not participate in Voicethread mediated feedback helped to empower the students to take an active role in at least part of their own and others' assessment. This shift in power away from the tutor, which is sometimes difficult to achieve, was clearly aided by the Voicethread service. However the design of the peer assessment activity itself and in particular the engagement with assessment criteria were also instrumental in relinquishing responsibility to the students.

Returning to Anderson's big ideas (2007), the class participatory culture in evidence here can be viewed as strongly linked to some ideas and more weakly to others, as follows;

- **User generated content**: there was a strong sense of ownership connected to the production of the students' highly personal digital stories
- **The power of the crowd**: this was less of a contributory factor in peer interactions as students were all novice assessors and tended to treat each others' expertise with a healthy scepticism.
- **Architecture of participation:** students made only modest use of the commenting facilities in Voicethread. Most feedback was left as a short isolated text comments. Typically no conversations grew around the works in progress.
- **Openness**: there was a strong and significant willingness to share works in progress with others.

The student groups also displayed some of the characteristics of participatory online cultures as described by Jenkins (2006). They seemed to develop a sense of social responsibility in particular for the learning of others possibly driven in part by a transfer of control and power from tutor to students. However no informal mentoring relationships were observed probably because the group was fairly homogeneous in terms of their experience of the task and of being assessors. The impact of this peer assessment activity on student learning and personal development is difficult to determine however there are indications that these might extend beyond the local context.

6 Conclusions

Two cohorts of undergraduate students and their tutor successfully adopted the Voicethread web 2.0 service to create multimedia digital story productions and to mediate peer feedback interactions in support of their refinement. This peer assessment activity empowered students to take on partial responsibility for their own and others assessment and supported critical engagement with a set of assessment criteria. Both the characteristics of the web 2.0 service and the design of the peer assessment activity contributed to a particular class culture of participation which differed from expectations shaped by informal use of web 2.0 services and analyses of its pedagogic potential. Hence we might be well advised to view with caution the rhetoric surrounding web 2.0 and its potential for catalysing radical change in formal learning contexts and look rather for synergies between new web 2.0 technologies and well researched and rehearsed pedagogic practices such a peer assessment.

Acknowledgements

This work was carried out in collaboration with the students and Gabriel Edwards, the course tutor. It was funded by the University of Bath Teaching Development Fund.

References

Anderson, P. (2007) "What is Web 2.0? Ideas, technologies and implications for education", *JISC Technology and Standards Watch*. pp14-26.

Boud, D. (1994) "The move to self assessment: liberation or a new mechanism for oppression?", *In SCUTREA Conference proceedings,* pp10-13.

Burden, K. and Atkinson, S. (2008) "Evaluating pedagogical affordances of media sharing web 2.0 technologies: a case study", Paper read at *the* Ascilite conference, Melbourne, Australia

Cho, K. and MacAuthur, C. (2010) "Student revision with peer and expert reviewing", *Learning and Instruction,* Vol. 20. No. 4, pp328-338

Davies, P. (2008) "The *computerized peer-assessment of digital storytelling in higher education*", In: Khandia, F. (ed.). 12th CAA International Computer Assisted Assessment Conference Proceedings pp79-94, Lougborough University, July.

Downes, S. (2007) "Learning Networks in Practice". In *Emerging Technologies for Learning* , Vol. 2, Chapter 2. Becta.

Elliot, B. (2007) "Assessment 2.0", [online], SQA, http://wiki.cetis.ac.uk/images/d/de/Assessment_2_v2.pdf

Falchikov, N. (2007) "The Place of Peers in Learning and Assessment". In *Rethinking Assessment in Higher Education: Learning for the Longer term*. Eds. D. Boud and N. Falchikov, pp128-143. Routledge, Oxon.

Falchikov, N. (2005) *Improving Assessment through Student Involvement*. Routledge, London.

Jenkins, H. (2006) *Confronting the Challenges of Participatory Culture*. MIT Press, USA.

Lenhart, A. and Madden, M. (2005) "Teen Content Creators and Consumers", [online] Washington, DC: Pew Internet & American Life Project. http://www.pewinternet.org/pdfs/PIP_Teens_Content_Creation.pdf

Mejias, U. (2005). A nomad's guide to learning and social software. [online] *The Knowledge tree: An e-journal of learning innovation.* http://knowledgetree.flexiblelearning.net.au/edition07/download/la_mejias.pdf

McDrury, J. & Alterio, M. (2003) *Learning Through StoryTelling in Higher Education: using reflection and experience to improve learning*. Kogan Page, London.

McLoughlin, C. & Lee, M. (2007) "Social software and participatory learning: Pedagogical choices with technology affordances in the Web 2.0 era". In *ICT: Providing choices for learners and learning.Proceedings Ascilite Singapore 2007*

Nicol, D, J. & Macfarlane-Dick, D. (2006) "Formative assessment and self-regulated learning: A model and seven principles of good feedback practice", Studies in Higher Education, Vol. 31, No. 2, pp199-218

Selwyn, N. (2008) "Education 2.0? Designing the web for Teaching and Learning". *TLRP. London, Institute of Education*

Stake, R. E. (2000) "Case studies", In *Handbook of qualitative research*, Eds. N. K. Denzin and Y. S. Lincoln, 2nd edition, pp237–247. Thousand Oaks, CA, Sage.

Walker, S., Jameson, J. & Ryan, M. (2010) "Skills and Strategies for E-learning", In *Rethinking Learning for a Digital Age: How learners are shaping their own experiences*. Eds. R. Sharpe, H. Beetham & S. de Freitas Routledge, Oxon

.

Playing With Fire: Kindling Learning Through Mobile Gaming

Michael Power[1], S Daniel[1], Silvie Barma[1] and Rob Harrap[2]
[1]Laval University, Canada
[2]Queen's University, Canada

Editorial commentary
As the previous chapter emphasized, building a mixed-reality serious game of the adventure genre makes it difficult to foster collaborative activities. In the strategy genre, Power, Daniel, Barma and Harrap present in this chapter a serious game project in which gameplay was deeply grounded in collaboration amongst players. The game is both mobile and context aware, with Laval University's campus being transformed into a playfield for teams equipped with mobile devices for an augmented reality competition. Thus this chapter provides multiple insightful answers on how to develop the social dimension of mobile immersive games: shared real life or digital artefacts using geo-caching (finding real hidden objects thanks to their GPS coordinates), geo-tagging (adding GPS information to photos and other digital), and designing game play got players with different but complementary roles. The main benefit of such games lies in providing them with an immersive, reactive and interactive pedagogical experience, making learning fun and sustainable as learners interpret their roles from an actor's posture.

Abstract: Mobile learning is increasingly commonplace at all levels of education as well as in the workplace. Its ubiquity, immediacy, flexibility and especially its strong motivational power are such that large-scale adoption is likely imminent, especially as smart phone technology becomes affordable. Another emerging trend is mobile gaming, a looming multimillion dollar industry following in the footsteps of the billion–dollar gaming industry. Furthermore, gaming industry giants such as UBI-SOFT predict that 'serious gaming' will be the fastest-growing segment of the industry over the next decade. In this article, we present a project which is innovative and unique in combining M-learning, M-gaming and Serious Gaming within the purvey of science and technology High School curricula implementing 3D, Augmented Reality (AR) technology.

Keywords: mobile gaming, augmented reality, geomatics

1   Introduction

"The mind is not a vessel to be filled, but a fire to be kindled." Plutarch

Until recently, mobile gaming was simply defined as being able to play a game anywhere, anytime using a handheld device: there was no clear or specific relationship between where the player was geographically located and what was happening *in-game*. New geomatics-based, serious mobile simulation gaming prototypes are immersive, reactive and interactive and exploit gamer localisation, i.e. geopositioning, geo-tagging and geo-caching, and frequently engage students as both players and authors, thereby contributing to emerging socially-constructed networks of sites and artefacts. Although the scope of research in this project is necessarily wide-ranging, this article will focus specifically on the educational technology-based, game scenario design activities under development. The educational issues being addressed by researchers involve serious gaming, mobile gaming, simulation gaming design, scenario-building and interdisciplinary research. Moreover, given the wealth of research studies being generated by the GeoEduc3D project and its group of international researchers, this article will focus primarily on the initial design and development activities currently being undertaken by the team during the gaming prototype-building phase.

The methodology implemented in this study is based on the *design research* approach (Brown, 1992; Kelly, 2004). Design research focuses not only on products generated during gaming design sessions but also on the entire design process involving numerous 'microcycles' (Bell, 2004) that include all the design steps, everything from initial design to prototyping, to beta-testing and pilots on through to delivery and follow-up assessment. As a result, GeoEduc3D gaming prototype design involves intensive in-field, observation-based, iterative data collection. Gaming design sessions are followed up by debriefing sessions conducted among researchers and graduate students and results from such are reinvested in prototype-building.

Current results relate to the design phase of the project and, more specifically, highlight gaming-scenario, game mechanics and character identification and role association, situating prototype design status, showcasing current developments and identifying problem areas and technological limits encountered.

2 Context: Serious gaming and M-gaming

Serious gaming has become a major influence in education since Abt first coined the term in 1970. It is now the object of serious worldwide conferences (www.seriousgames.org; www.digra.org), serious publishing (Gee, 2003; Jenkins, 2002; Saywer, 2002) and serious money, over 1.7 billion in Canada alone in 2008 (www.gamasutra.com). Realizing the potential for serious learning, researchers and graduate students from Canada, France, the Netherlands, the UK and the USA are taking part in a project – *GeoEduc3D* – aimed at designing and developing educational games which implements state-of-the-art geospatial technology and explores thematic issues specifically relevant to a teenager public, such as climate change and sustainable development. Through immersive, reactive and interactive gaming, GeoEduc3D's purpose is grounded in mobility. Until recently, mobile gaming was simply defined as being able to play a game anywhere using a handheld device. Now, more recent developments in the field of *M-learning* (mobile learning) and *M-gaming* (mobile gaming) are exploiting gamer localisation (i.e. location-based games), geo-tagging and geo-caching (Klopfer, 2008). Geo-tagging refers to associating photographs and captions with specific locations. Collections of photographs can then be retrieved and viewed on-the-fly. Geo-caching refers to finding hidden objects given basic coordinates and a GPS device. The goal may be, for instance, to retrieve a code or to leave a note for fellow gamers, thereby contributing to an emerging socially-constructed network of sites and objects. Geo-tagging offers students the opportunity to not only access remote locations with culturally relevant 3D virtual artefacts attached but also to contribute to the collection using digital cameras and GPS devices. Based on an educational objectives-based selection of sites, the serious games thus developed promote both physical activity and socio-cultural awareness which have the potential to enhance and improve existing educational curricula.

Location-based (or location-enabled) gaming offers new possibilities for enriching games and enhancing gamer playing/learning by taking advantage of global positioning capabilities and actual spatial context (Penn State Urban Gaming Club http://www.pennstateugc.org/). Currently, the cell phone is the most wide-spread platform for mobile gaming (Wisniewski & Morton, 2005). Other technologies are also being used, such as Personal Digital Assistant, equipped with GPS and Wi-Fi, Bluetooth or radio connexions (GSM, CDMA, etc.) (Inman, 2006). However, the technological framework of these platforms usually limits the range of games and interest in such due to the limited display size, low computational capabilities and available interaction tools (e.g. interaction with other gamers through instant messaging) (Ardito, Costabile, Lanziloti & Pederson, 2007). However, systems such as Nintendo's DS and Sony's PSP game consoles – currently the most advanced handheld platforms available on the market – offer the best prospective in terms of truly immersive and interactive game implementation. For instance, in Japan, external GPS and camera are provided with the PSP console (Shoemaker, 2006). Yet, up until now, there have been no truly location-based games designed for these platforms, the consoles not yet being fitted for mobility. But this situation is quickly changing as seen by innovations shown at the CES 2008 convention (CES, 2008). For instance, the designer of *Plundr* (http://plundr.playareacode.com/), the first PC location-based game, has adapted its game to *Nintendo DS* console (Miller, 2007; see also http://en.oreilly.com/where2009/, http://playareacode.com/ and R4DS http://www.r4ds.cn/, namely the *Homebrew* platform). This version is the first location-based game, purposely designed for use with a handheld, mobile console. In sum, the emergence of new products on the market which are adapted to localisation stem from new research with regard to the effective, robust, interactive and real-time exploitation of gamer mobility.

3   Main research objective

Our overall objective is to stimulate student interest in, and deepen their understanding of, geomatic methods and technology through geomatics-enabled mobile games supporting targeted learning in science and technology, such as on climate change and sustainable development. The scope of research is thus wide-ranging, from educational problem-solving activities development to geomatically-supported, technological solution-building.

4 Knowledge and skills acquisition, Curricula reform in Québec and GeoEduc3D

In a recent report published by the *Canadian Council on Learning* (2007), learning among young adults has been identified as a major issue and one of its key concerns. The GeoEduc3D project, by specifically targeting young adult learning, is contributing to better understanding the challenges involved in knowledge and skills acquisition within this learning community, in defining new, innovative and especially relevant learning solutions and in meeting the needs of 21st-century learners. The augmented reality solutions implemented in the project, by creating learning environments which are entertaining, even thrilling, represent a practical approach to meeting learner needs while fostering increased levels of cognitive competency (Shelton, 2002). With regard to learner needs and desirable competency development, the project is focussing more on skills development than on actual content-based knowledge gamers acquire from playing a game. From an educational point of view, critical skills that are generally targeted by stakeholders (Fink, 2003) are:

- Critical thinking
- Team work
- Communicative abilities
- Problem-solving
- Visual and spatial thinking (spatial awareness)

The current Curricula Reform in Québec is aiming at cross-disciplinary competencies as promoted by the Department of Education. Within such and in connection with GeoEduc3D, three main science and technology-based competencies are prioritised. Hence, teachers are encouraged to promote the emergence of a basic scientific and technological culture among students. The three sought-after competencies require that a student

- "seeks answers or solutions to scientific or technological problems";

- "makes the most of his/her knowledge of science and technology" and
- "communicates in the languages used in science and technology".

In light of this first competency (1), the GeoEduc3D gaming prototype under development (described below) situates students as members of a team tasked with undertaking learning activities linked to real-world, energy consumption and conservation problems.

As for the second competency (2), the student "makes the most of his/her knowledge of science and technology", students are required to develop their capacity to conceptualize and to transfer learning skills from one discipline to another. Students engaging in GeoEduc3D games use realistic tools and resources to make decisions that have an immediate impact. However, because these activities are entirely game-based, no negative consequences ensue and students can replay scenarios as often as they wish, thereby learning from their mistakes (and especially those of others) as well as transferring knowledge acquired from one problematic situation to another.

Finally, as for the 3rd competency, « (the student) communicates in the languages used in science and technology", within the GeoEduc3D game scenarios, students are required to analyze data, design solutions, develop these solutions by estimating required resources, comparing data from various potential solutions, implementing the best solutions and assessing results, while communicating with their team members on an ongoing basis using both verbal and written communications.

5   Game scenario design and development

The most advanced GeoEduc3D prototype currently under development is a mobile version of the desktop game developed during the first year of the project, *Energy wars-Rise of the Chimera*. It is a "serious mobile simulation game"; it is serious in that there are activities that require skills and knowledge development; it is mobile in that players are free, even required to move about a wide area; it is a simulation in that it is located in the real world, on campus at Laval University (Canada) and, finally, it is also a game in that there will be winners and losers, involving a race against time and obstacles. The original version of this game was developed under the stewardship of Associate Director Rob Harrap of Queen's University (Canada). The mobile version is being headed by Project Director Sylvie Daniel and Associate Director-Education Michael Power at Laval University. This version of the game prototype includes role-playing and the goal of the game is to capture and retrofit building on campus in order to improve energy efficiency. Players can access virtual engineers, experts in energy consumption, who move randomly about camp controlling access to the buildings. As they invest the campus, they are facing a competing team who can plant misleading information that may induce them to waste their precious resources. The Queen's team suggested we think of *Energy Wars* as a kind of *Monopoly* designed for sustainable development[1].

The Queen's University game prototype used a *LidAR*-based, 3D model of the campus which had previously been scanned by a mobile *LidAR* unit (the same unit also scanned all of the Laval University campus). *LidAR* (Light Detection And Ranging) is a "a measuring system that detects and locates objects on the same principle as radar but uses light from a laser" www.wordnetweb.princeton.edu/perl/webwn. The data collected allows for precise millimeter-by-millimeter geolocation and, when used in gaming applications, provides an exact overlap of the virtual, on-screen environment and the real one, thereby enhancing player immersion in the game.

However, the precision of the scanners used was such that screen resolution was very high. To compensate for this, i.e. to reduce screen resolution to manageable levels for mobile gaming purposes, *Google SketchUP* was used to design to-scale mock-ups based on the *LidAR* data. The main technical problem was, since *LidAR* captures millions of dots, the resulting data is simply to voluminous for the gaming motors we were prototyping to manage. Furthermore, because *LidAR* data is comprised simply of dots and not complete surfaces, more geometric modeling and processing was required using *Google SketchUP* to be able to identify building and other elements in the environment. The overall technical (geomatics-related) objective is to incorporate, into the gaming scenario, 3D objects that react

---

[1] http://geoeduc3d.scg.ulaval.ca/index.php?page=nouvelles&id=12

to player movement so that players can freely navigate on campus using their mobile devices while accessing a 3D screen view.

6   Serious mobile gaming scenario prototype

Reference document : Secondary Cycle 2 – Science & Technology Curriculum

Students: from ages 14 to 16

Learning goal: The serious side of gaming aims at developing, as mentioned above, the 3 science & technology-related competencies, that is, developing knowledge with regard to scientific and technological concepts and related skills allowing them to apply a scientific approach when investigating a problem while effectively communicating with team members in order to 'capture' on-campus buildings and to take steps towards improving their energy consumption. Through an in-depth analysis of the environmental issues in play, teams are expected to identify the potential and plausible impact of their decisions on said environment.

Environmental problem: the world energy challenge

Main Concepts: energy production and use, carbon-based resources, materials, renewable energy, system and technologies, energy transformation.

Main elements: the prototype design team is integrating the following elements into the game scenario: the buildings on campus are not energy-wise; budgets are limited ; there are various environmental restrictions ; synchronization of actions/communications between team members; definition and elaboration of building-capture strategies and problem-solving activities in relationship to energy-saving measures; development of proposal templates for communicating recommendations to decision-makers.

Areas of expertise
- Environmental safeguards and energy consumption:
- Environment-based knowledge (based on environmental impact studies)

- Responsible energy consumption and use of public goods and services (based on energy consumption analysis reports)
- Social, economic and ethical aspects of conscience-building with regard to energy consumption (based on consumer energy consumption studies
- Building a viable environment in the perspective of sustainable development (based on environmental impact studies)

Player roles and expertise:

- 1 – Commander: in charge of Headquarters (may be the teacher), has access to a desktop or laptop computer and coordinates in-game player action and (re)distributes information received from the field. Some aspects of the game are currently 'closed' (predetermined by the design team), some aspects are 'open' (player designated).
- 2 – Communications officer (Comms): in charge of all communications between all players (including the Commander). Moves about on campus with an 'enhanced mobile unit' (Android ou Iphone with full functions).
- 3 – Scout: in charge of advance reconnoitering, building ID and initial energy assessment. Moves about on campus with a 'limited mobile unit' (Android ou Iphone with some functions).
- 4 –Construction expert (3 in number): using energy-saving and environmental impact-based data, this expert is in charge of analyzing detailed energy consumption profiles for each building and making norm-based assessment retrofitting appraisals in light of the recommendations of the other experts. Moves about on campus with a limited mobile unit, as directed by Comms.
- 5 –Environmental expert: using construction norm- and energy saving-based data, this expert is in charge of analyzing the potential environmental impact of recommendations made by the other experts. Moves about on campus with a limited mobile unit and as directed by Comms.
- 6 – Expert in energy-saving materials and devices. Se déplace sur le terrain avec une plate-forme mobile (Android ou Iphone).

7   Example of a scenario under development

The year is 2015. As part of its 5-Year Sustainable Development Plan, Laval University has decided it needs to makes fundamental changes to its energy consumption patterns, completely reversing its current pattern form a fossil-fuel, energy-consuming community (a city within a city) to a green, energy-producing community. As a result, groups of students in Architecture, Civil Engineering and Environmental Studies have been tasked with designing a new campus including both physical and virtual components, services and structures, including recommendations for achieving, in the short term, energy efficiency and, in the mid-term, complete **Energy Independence** + i.e. returning energy to the provincial "Energy Grid", promoting, as an overriding consideration, sustainable 'green' community behaviour among its members. Using precise geolocation-based coordinates, teams must first locate buildings on campus and then collect and analyze their current energy consumption profiles. The experts must identify potential energy-saving measures (through construction, reconstruction or retrofitting) with low environmental impact and produce a report identifying trade-offs and presenting alternatives. As a team 'captures' a building (by investing in energy-saving measures), it is added to their campus map. In addition, in order to successfully capture buildings, teams must compare their environmental impact and energy-saving measures with those of other teams. Therefore, in some cases, building that were originally captured by one team can be taken over by another team. Ultimately, the team with the best 'package' wins.

Preparatory mission: Exploratory and discovery-based and, teams carry out this mission to learn about the game mechanics and various roles and types of interactions between team members. To get started, teams receive an incomplete map of the campus on an *iPhone* or *Android*-based smartphone. They can see individual building locations and dimensions as well as spaces between buildings which may or may not be true to real-world specifications. There also see what looks like damaged buildings and buildings under construction and open spaces where there may or may not be buildings or outdoor facilities. Before team members spread out, the *Commander* sets out a preliminary plan (path-to-follow across campus) to maximize efficiency, taking into consideration the time available for this mission. As the team sets out, for the *Scout* at the fore, data starts pouring into Headquarters (HQ) via *Comms*. In some cases, the *Scout* encounters, in some cases, new or existing buildings, in others, empty spaces or damaged buildings or newly-renovated buildings, public spaces or sports facilities. Based on geolocated vectors, he *Scout* confirms or denies building ID and locations and updates the map, creating virtual geotags on-site and providing such to Comms who then transmits it on to the *Experts*. The *Experts*, following instructions from *Comms*, find (by moving around the buildings) and access the *Scout's* geotags as well as other geocached, expert data available on-site. They start compiling data on construction needs, energy-saving measures or environmental considerations and, once they've uploaded their specific data to HQ, move on to the next building as directed by *Comms*. Together with the *Scout*, they thus complete the map with real-time, updated data and return to HQ with a general development plan for a debriefing with the *Commander*.

8   Game interface development

Parallel to scenario development, a small team of educational and geomatics researchers and graduate students are designing the game interface. In Figures 1 and 2, the registration page interface is presented where players choose their role and then access any one of three campus maps, a 2D real-time satellite image, a 3D, ground-view virtual map or a real-time player location map (showing where team members are currently located on campus).

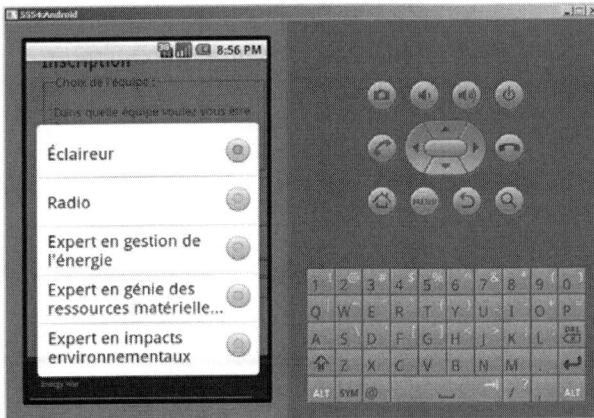

Figure 1: Registration interface page (T. Butzbach, GéoÉduc3D)

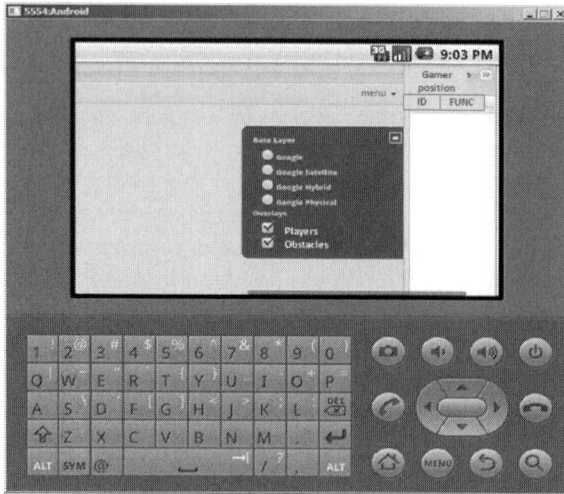

Figure 2: Map selection and options page (T. Butzbach, GéoÉduc3D)

Figure 3 shows the Commander's and Scout's geopositioned, satellite view of one section of the Laval University campus.

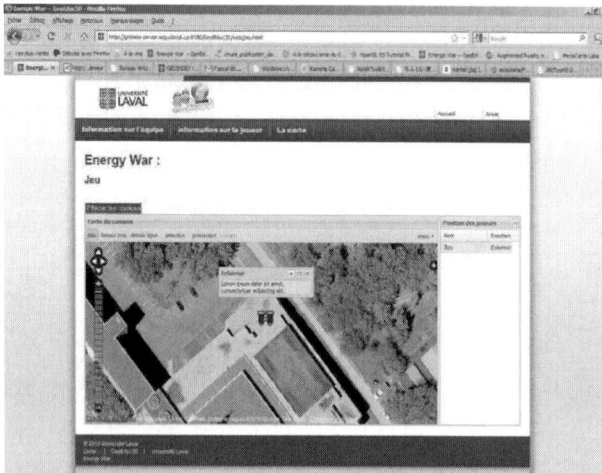

Figure 3: Commander's and Scout's satellite view of one section of campus (T. Butzbach, GéoÉduc3D)

Then, in Figure 4, is the same interface as in Figure 3 but using but using *Google Maps* in plan mode.

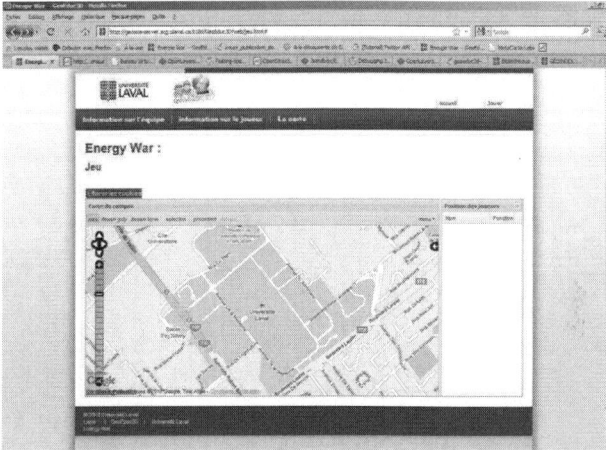

Figure 4: Commander's and Scout's *Google Maps* view of one section of campus (T. Butzbach, GéoÉduc3D)

The Scout, using his Augmented Reality-enhanced device, can see obstacles *in situ* that no one else can see. His key role is to keep the Commander informed of map updates as they are observed and recorded in order to give his team a tactical advantage. In Figure 5, a mock-up of an AR-enhanced screen shot is presented showing both distances and real-time team member positions on campus.

Figure 5: AR-enhanced screen showing both distances and team member positions (T. Butzbach, GéoÉduc3D)

In Figure 6, the Scout geotags in-field observations, discoveries and/or obstacles as they are encountered and transmits this information to the Commander who, using these real-time updates, is tasked with planning player moves, thereby developing an overall strategy for his/her team to efficiently and effectively capture as many of the buildings on campus as possible.

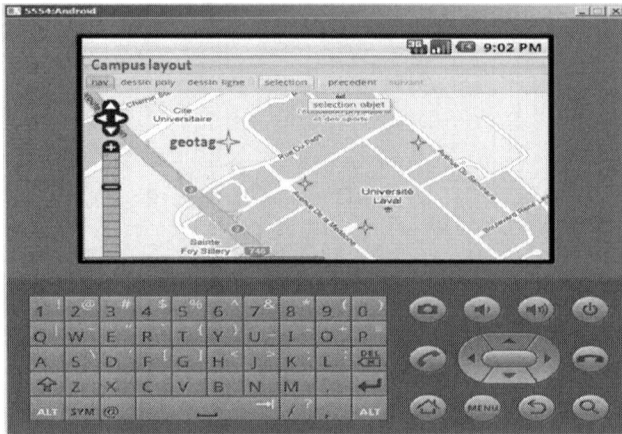

Figure 6: AR-enhanced screen showing both distances and team member positions (T. Butzbach, GéoÉduc3D)

The screen in Figure 7 shows the interface the experts access and the options they have to upload applications on-the-fly that will be of particular help in playing the specific role and in carrying out the tasks that they have been assigned. They also have a logbook (*journal*) for writing up technical data on building upgrades and retrofits which they can share real-time with all team members. They will also have access to a scientific calculator for budgeting purposes.

Team communications will take place via *Twitter*. Figure 8 shows the comms interface and a real-time exchange (in French) between the Commander and Comms. Figure 9 shows the exchange log interface.

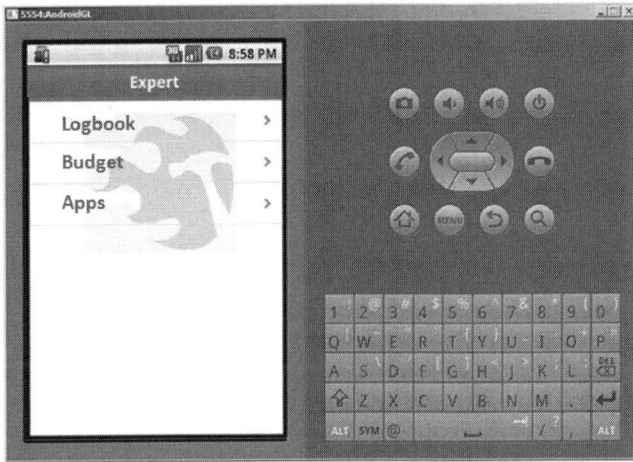

Figure 7: Expert access interface and options (T. Butzbach, GéoÉduc3D)

Figure 8: Team comms interface via *Twitter* (M.-A. Dumont, GéoÉduc3D)

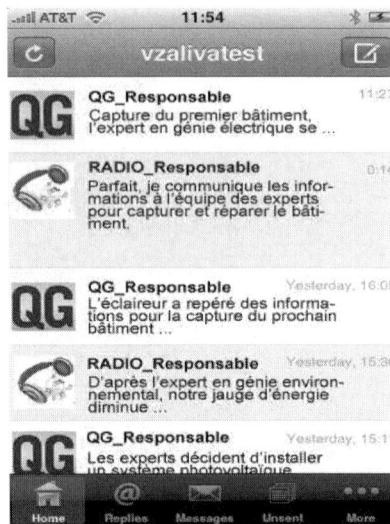

Figure 9: Exchange log interface (M.-A. Dumont, GéoÉduc3D)

9 Discussion

One of the strengths of the GeoEduc3D team has been its interdisciplinary nature. Interdisciplinariness in this project has required close and deep collaboration between researchers and graduate students and various fields of study but especially a fundamental acceptance of differing points of view in order to reach a common representation of the serious mobile simulation game under development. Interdisciplinariness is an integrating practice which is of special interest when tackling problems which require a global approach. Fourez, Englebert-Leconte & Mathy (1997, p.84) state that, « narrowly interpreted, [it is] a construction of representations of the world that are structured, organised and based on a human project (or on a problem requiring a solution), within a specific context and for specific individuals in mind, calling upon various and different disciplines in order to arrive at an original result which depends less on the disciplines represented than on the project itself" (free translation by the authors).

The educational team was not, in the beginning, specifically interested in or even fully aware of hardware affordances or software programming to be done. We were mostly concerned with developing gaming scenarios that **mobile**, allowing players to play outside the classroom, as well as **serious**, in that they lent themselves to curricula- based learning and (herein lied the main challenge) **fun** to play, in that children would enjoy playing them. Interdisciplinariness became a reality only when the gaming scenario went from an educational storyboard to a technical prototype involving technical and technological resources, functions and affordances. We realized that there were pros and cons to completely closed environments as well as to completely open environments. On the one hand, a closed environment would likely require a level and intensity of programming that was obviously not within our grasp or budget. On the other hand, an open environment with little structure may leave players bewildered and confused, with too many choices to make and too little to 'go on' once engaged in the game. In the end, it appeared likely that the end result would be a hybrid environment, with some aspects left open (to enhance player engagement) and some intentionally closed (to provide enough structure for forward momentum in the game).

Furthermore, it was interesting to observe how educators and geomaticians identify their respective research interests and conduct their respective research. A significant gap between such was immediately observed when the latter informed the former of specific information that had to be developed in the scenario and provided to them when programming the scenario. Many items had 'fallen between the cracks' so to speak, in that neither the educators nor the geomaticians had initially thought of developing this information since it was of little immediate interest to either group. However, once the scenario had been designed and when the team was tasked with developing the actual game mechanics, this is when the team realized that having this information was crucial to moving the game prototype forward. For instance, the educators had identified various player tasks linked to developing specific competencies which turned out to be too time- and effort- consuming to develop, technically speaking. Thus ensued a weekly series of meetings to 'hash out' the details. The overall experience has been highly beneficial in helping the entire team fully understand the exact nature of Interdisciplinariness in project development.

In closing, here are some comments made by a team member (part of the education team) reflecting about design and development activities undertaken over the past few months:

"Technological affordances (or lack thereof) were front and fore-most during our joint (education-geomatics) team discussions. We had to constantly reassess, rethink even our competency-related tasks in light of what the geomatics team was actually able to do. When we were designing these activities, we were not really preoccupied with what they would entail from a programming standpoint; we were mostly worried about making the game educational but also fun to play.

So we faced the ongoing challenge of redesigning our scenario and related activities in order to take into account difficulties encountered during the software programming, continuously being called upon to find alternatives or, at times, even having to completely re-design some elements so as to move the prototype forward.

So the researchers and graduate students working in education and in geomatics had to constantly adapt to one another during this de-sign-development overlap phase. Interestingly, we were often at loggerheads, not all aware of or sensitive to the same kinds of obstacles. For instance, when discussing concepts such as fantasy, strategy, rewards, competition, player environment control, educators often saw such issues through what they termed an ethical prism whereas geomaticians frequently saw them essentially as technical choices. Neither view was by itself sufficient to produce a working prototype but both were essential in doing so."

10 Conclusion

In this article, we have striven to document the ongoing work in the GeoEduc3D project, namely work involving the mobile, serious gaming scenario prototyping that has occurred over the past six months by a composite team of educational and geomatics researchers and graduate students. Few studies have documented this kind and level of interdisciplinary collaboration in the field of mobile serious simulation gaming, especially with regard to sustainably green development and curricula-anchored competency development. The GeoEduc3D project is currently at the end of the first prototype design phase and has moving into the development phase (with frequent, iterative returns to the design phase). Achieving equilibrium between playability and serious learning remains elusive as an ultimate goal yet we do feel some progress has been made in this direction.

We also feel that significant progress is being made with regard to advancing interdisciplinary research and development. Indeed, harmonizing the mastery of the integration geospatial data while appropriating scientific and technological concepts by means of interactional dynamics between players and competing teams is a huge step. It involves accommodating a vast array of research interests (even whims) as expressed by the researchers and graduate students engaged in this process. Moreover, the challenge of first imagining and designing activities that implement augmented reality and then developing them appears to have been the biggest one yet. Interestingly, zones of convergence between project actors did emerge, as did a workable prototype which we will soon be testing (Sept-Oct. 2010) and which will bring us one step closer to our next goal: using it in the field with High School students and their teachers.

References
Ardito, C., Costabile, M.F., Lanziloti, R. & Pederson, T. (2007). Making Dead History Come Alive Through Mobile Game-Play. CHI 2007, April 28 – May 3 2007, San Jose, CA.

Bell, P. (2004). On the theoretical breadth of design-based research. Educational Psychologist, 39(4), 243-253.

Brown, A. L. (1992). Design Experiments: Theoretical and Methodological Challenges in

Creating Complex Interventions in Classroom Settings. The Journal of the Learning Sciences, 2(2), 141-178.

CES 2008 http://www.cesweb.org/ (Retrieved 12/12/2008).

Canadian Council on Learning (2007). État de l'apprentissage au Canada : Pas le temps de s'illusionner. Rapport sur l'apprentissage au Canada 2007. Ottawa, Canada.

Fink, D. (2003). Creating Significant Learning. Jossey-Bass, San Francisco.

Gee J. (2003) What video games have to teach us about learning and literacy. Palgrave Macmillan, New York.

Inman, M. (2006). Mobile Games Superimpose Virtual Fun on the Real World. National Geographic News, October 16, 2006, http://news.nationalgeographic.com (Retrieved 12/01/2008)

Jenkins, H. (2002). Game Theory: Digital Renaissance. Technology Review. MIT. March 29, 2002.

Kelly, A. E. (2004). Design Research in Education: Yes, but is it a methodological? The Journal of the Learning Sciences, 13(1), 115-128.

Klopfer., E. (2008). Handheld Simulation Games Augmenting Learning and Reality. Cambridge, Mass.: MIT Press.

Miller, R. (2007). Plundr, first location-based DS game. Where 2.0. Conference, Joystiq, June 4. http://www.joystiq.com/2007/06/04/plundr-first-location-based-ds-game-debuts-at-where-2-0/ (Retrieved 12/04/2008)

Sawyer, B. (2002). Serious games: improving public policy through game-based learning and simulation. Foresight and Governance Project, Woodrow Wilson International Center for Scholars.

Shelton, B. (2002). Augmented Reality and Education: Current Projects and the Potential for Classroom Learning. New Horizons for Learning. December, http://www.newhorizons.org (Retrieved 12/03/2008)

Shoemaker, B. (2006). TGS06 : Kutaragi talks PSP3 at keynote. Gamespot News, September 21. Retrieved 12/01/2008: http://www.gamespot.com/news/6158144.html (Retrieved 12/07/2008)

Wisniewski, D. & Morton D. (2005). 2005 Mobile Games White Paper. Game Developers Conference. San Francisco 7-11 March, International Game Developers Association Report, 55 p.

Designing Mobile Gaming Narratives for Guided Discovery Learning in Interactive Environments

Ling-yi Huang
National Chengchi University, Taipei, Taiwan

Editorial commentary

In this chapter Ling-yi presents an approach to designing a new breed of serious game. While the Internet of things is still emerging, what some analysts are calling Web 3.0, Ling-yi is already previewing the use of augmented reality in educational games ... games that take root in our real environment with overlapping digital content. Last generation mobile devices together with 4G networks solve most of the technological constraints in this regard. The main issue to succeed in this endeavor lies in creating a mixed-reality educational experience to obtain positive changes in learning outcomes. Indeed, this is an issue common to discovery-based learning environments in which learners experience a lack of guidance. Ling-yi reaches into interactive narrative theories to solve the issue, identifying amongst the different narrative models that both provide guidance and are applicable in an environmental based game design. A combination of three models is distinguished as most suitable for the serious game experience, covering the definition of the main plotline, the possible emergent stories, as well as embedded stories. Finally, a critical analysis of the adventure game Façade illustrates the application of the model. Ling-yi concludes with recommendations for designers of mobile gaming narratives for an environment-based game, recalling the importance of including even wrong choices into the game play to enable a learn-by-error experience.

Abstract: The research question of this paper is "How to build a narrative-centered interactive environment for mobile game learning"? It attempts to achieve two purposes: first, to provide suggestions for designing mobile games in interactive environments and second, to explore the possible learning outcomes from mobile gaming. The research method used is textual analysis of the case "Façade", an interactive environmental adventure game. The findings suggest that the flow chart, the hidden story and the braided plot are the best suited narrative texts for adventure games to guide learners in narrative-centered environments. Moreover, the possible learning outcomes from mobile adventure games could be guided discovery learning. In conclusion, this study suggests that in mobile adventure game design, teachers should consider which location is an important node that every learner has to go through. In each node, teachers should provide some choices, including wrong ones. Teachers also need to consider different possible ending scenarios according to learners' self-construction. Finally, teachers have to explain why different learners have different results. Further studies can also apply the theories mentioned above on stories of different genres to design different adventure games for various purposes.

Keywords: global positioning satellites, location-based services, mobile interactive environments, adventure games, guided discovery learning, interactive narrative

1   Introduction

The fusion of Global Positioning Satellites (GPS), Location-based Services (LBS) and fourth-generation mobile internet featuring broadband wireless (4G) has opened many possibilities for new applications. According to Bădut(2004),

GPS helps the localization at ground level by correlating the positioning vectorial information simultaneously received from many specialized satellites. LBS refers to the automated services able to dynamically provide/supply information about a certain geo-spatial position: returning the actual location (of the user), or the position of a traced/followed objective (person, automobile, maritime/aerial ship, cargo, building, object) relative to the current position of the user (Bădut, 2004).

Moreover, 4G has overcome the disadvantages of 3G such as weak response to availability, quality and cost expectations. 4G is different from

3G not only in the reasons mentioned above. 4G has some specific characteristics such as (Kanter, 2000):

- Other users, mobile devices and communication resources may
  become "visible" in an ad-hoc fashion, either by proximity or actively communicating.
- Entities (users, mobile artifacts and virtual objects) may exchange
  events that range beyond simple invitations to join a session all
  the way to manipulations of shared virtual objects.
- The communication conditions will vary between and even within
  access networks. This is especially the case where wireless communication is concerned.

In brief, GPS, LBS and 4G all together afford the possibilities for mobile
interactive environments. According to Kanter(2000), mobile interactive
environments can be called smart spaces or mobile interactive spaces. The
definition is as follows:

Smart spaces are ordinary environments equipped with sensing systems
(e.g. location, movement, visual, audio, etc.) that can perceive and react to
people and conversely, by instrumenting the physical world, enable people
to influence the virtual world (Kanter, 2000).

Although mobile interactive environments afford many new possibilities
for teaching and learning, how to use mobile devices to enhance learning
effects and what kind of learning effects might be enhanced in interactive
environments remain a topic to be discussed. Besides, most mobile learning studies focus on 3G. While few studies have started to discuss 4G applications in education such as the "The Mobile Interpreting Project" in
Finland (Koskinen, Veitonen, Laaksonen and Väänänen, 2005), it remains
an emergent topic to be discussed.

Moreover, narratives play an important role in combining pedagogy and
gaming into interactive environments. According to Bruner, narratives
could play an important role in discovery learning (Bruner, 1961). However, the lack of guidance in discovery learning is not sufficient to produce
positive changes in learning outcomes (Mayer, 2004, Kirschner, 2006). A
general mechanism to guide learners in the digital age is via interactive

narratives (Thomas and Young, 2007). Besides, narratives are also key elements in gaming. Smilansky and Shefatya (1990) pointed out that social dramatic play includes the following seven elements: imitative role play, make-believe with objects, make believe with actions and situations, interaction with people, verbal communication, persistence and narratives.

To sum up, the research question of this paper is "How to build a narrative-centered interactive environment for mobile game learning"? This paper attempts to achieve two purposes. The first one is to provide some suggestions for designing mobile gaming narratives in interactive environments and the second is to explore possible learning outcomes from gaming.

2   Adventure games and guided discovery learning

Adventure games can combine narratives with its educational purposes. According to Rollings & Adams (2003), the genres of games include action games, strategy games, role playing games, sports games, vehicle simulation, construction and management simulations, adventures games, artificial life and puzzle games. According to a review of the literature of educational video game design (Dondlinger, 2007), there are different learning outcomes resulting from different types of computer video game play. The learning outcomes include deduction and hypothesis testing, complex concepts and abstract thinking and finally visual and spatial processing. However, in this review, the relationship between game genres and learning outcomes are not specifically mentioned.

This study focuses on the genre of an adventure game and its desired learning outcomes. An adventure game is a software program which presents an artificial environment with which the user must interact in order to solve the problems presented in the game world (Cavallari, Hedberg and Harper 1992). It includes the following elements (Dillon, 2004):

- Game play is primarily driven by a narrative through which the player moves as the game progresses
- Other narrative-based art forms are used heavily, such as film, novels and comic books.
- The player generally controls the main character.

- Games are often based on quests or puzzles, which are solved through interaction with the game world and its objects – this is often integral to the game experience.
- Emphasis is on exploration, thought and problem-solving abilities over the fast reflexes of more action-styled games.

Adventure games and simulations may require students to interpret information, make judgments and predictions, determine further actions and promote spatial visualization, mapping and scale-drawing skills (NSW Department of Education, 1989: 37). Adventure games may enhance players' deduction and hypothesis testing, complex concepts and abstract thinking, visual and spatial processing.

The learning outcomes from adventure games may be similar to discovery learning. Discovery learning encourages students to learn by trial-and-error. Besides, it is widely believed that discovery learning offers much promise because students actively participate in problem-solving activities. Veermans (2002) points out five processes of discovery learning: (1) orientation, (2) hypothesis generation, (3) hypothesis testing, (4) conclusion and (5) regulative processes. According to the processes mentioned above, first, learners build their ideas of the domain and the learning environment. Second, learners start formulating hypotheses about the problems and questions of the domain. Third, learners design and execute experiments that put a hypothesis to the test, gather the data from the experiments, and interpret the results. Forth, learners decide whether the evidence is in line with predictions derived from the hypothesis, or identify discrepancies between evidence and predictions. Fifth, learners manage the work through the discovery learning processes described above. However, the lack of guidance in discovery learning is not sufficient to produce positive changes in learning outcomes (Mayer,2004 ; Kirschner, 2006). A general mechanism to guide learners in the digital age is via interactive narratives (Thomas and Young, 2007). Hence, this paper will use interactive narratives as a guidance mechanism for discovery learning.

3 Interactive narratives and guided discovery learning

How do narratives guide learners in an interactive environment? According to Ryan (2001: 246-256), there are nine kinds of interactive narrative texts. They are the complete graph, the network, the tree, the vector with side branches, the maze, the flow chart or directed network, the hidden story, the braided plot and the epic wandering. Below, each of these texts will be presented in more detail.

3.1 The complete graph

In the complete graph, every node is linked to every node and the user has total freedom to navigate. However, this design is not suitable for guiding learners because it doesn't provide enough information.

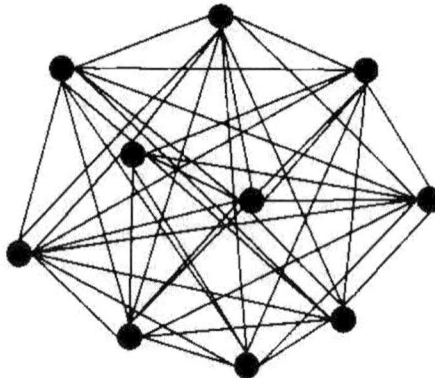

Figure 1: The complete graph (Ryan, 2001: 247)

3.2 The network

In the network, the user is neither totally free nor limited to a single course. However, it allows the user to navigate in circles. This may confuse the user. Hence, it is not suitable to guide learners.

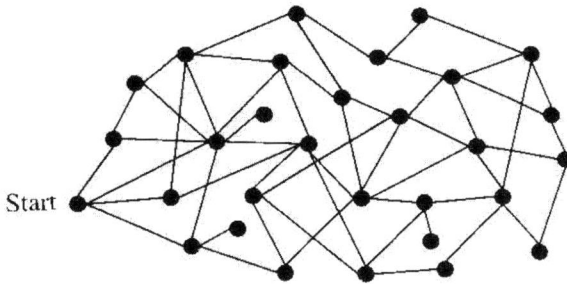

Figure 2: The network (Ryan, 2001: 248)

3.3   The tree

The design of the tree allows no circuits. However, each branch is strictly isolated from the others. It doesn't allow the learner to discover by trial and error. Hence, it is not suitable to guide learners.

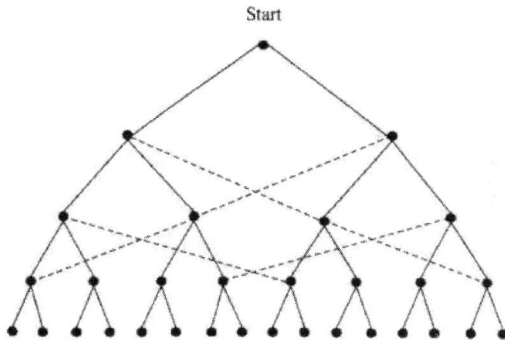

Figure 3: The tree (Ryan, 2001: 249)

3.4   The vector with side branches

In the vector with side branches, the text tells a determinate story in chronological order, but the structure of links enables the user to take short side trips. This design focuses on the sequence of the story and doesn't make good use of the environment. Hence, it is not suitable for environmental design.

163

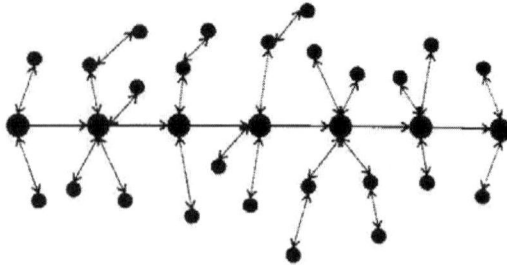

Figure 4: The vector with side branches (Ryan, 2001, 250)

3.5 The maze

The maze is characteristic of adventure games. This may or may not allow the user to run in circles. The node can be dead ends or allow backtracking. However, this story doesn't make good use of the environment and only allows some trial and error from the user. Hence, it is not suitable to guide the learner.

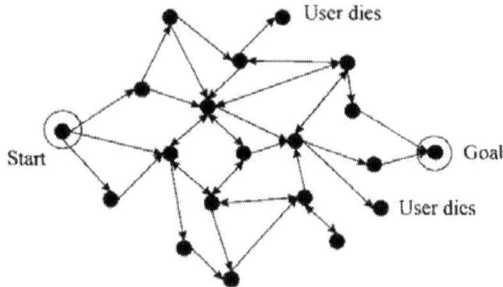

Figure 5: The maze (Ryan, 2001:251)

3.6 The flow chart or directed network

In the flow chart or directed network, the user no longer runs in a circle and meets the dead ends. The user may meet several important nodes which every user is required to pass through. In other nodes, the user can decide to go through it or not. This is suitable to guide the learner because it doesn't limit the user too much and there are also clues to guide the learner.

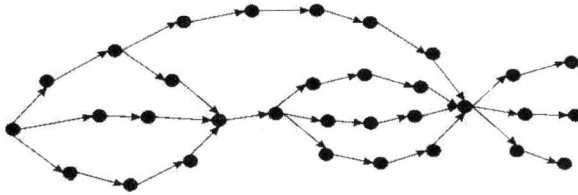

Figure 6: The flow chart or directed network (Ryan, 2001: 252)

3.7 The hidden story

This model consists of two stories. At the bottom there is the fixed, temporally directed story of the events to be reconstituted. On the top there is the temporal network of choices that determines the reader-detective's investigation of the case. Between the two there are dotted lines that link episodes of discovery in the top story to the discussed facts of the bottom story. This design is suitable for learners' discovery learning because it allows the learner to figure out what happened gradually from the navigation.

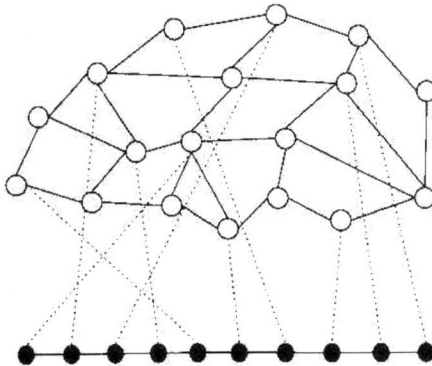

Figure 7: The hidden story (Ryan, 2001: 253)

3.8 The braided plot

This text shows how interactive mechanisms can be used to switch "windows" on a multi-stranded but determinated narrative. For example, from different characters' perspectives, the user can figure out what happened gradually. This is suitable to guide the learner since it requires the learner to explore different perspectives actively by himself.

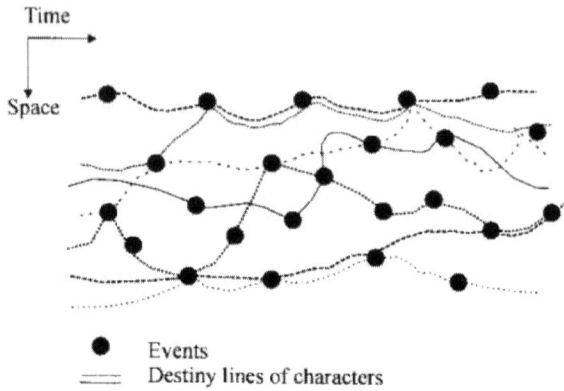

Figure 8: The braided plot (Ryan, 2001: 254)

3.9   Epic wandering

In epic wandering, the system takes control of the user's fate. The user can only navigate in a micro level story. Hence, no matter what the user chooses, the results won't be changed. This is not suitable to guide learners since the decision of the learner doesn't affect the results.

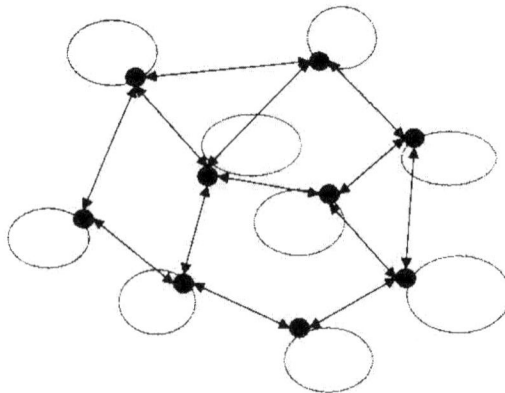

Figure 9: Epic wandering (Ryan, 2001: 255)

Above all, not all interactive narrative texts are suitable to be applied in GPS storytelling and to guide learners' discovery learning. The story should provide some clues but not confuse learners in a repeated circle. Hence, the complete graph, the network, the maze and the epic wandering are not suitable for guiding learners. Only the flow chart, the hidden story and the braided plot are suitable texts. Besides, the story should be applied in the environment to tell a story. This means that it is necessary to consider how to deploy interactive narratives in the environment.

4 Environmental design and guided discovery learning

Mobile adventure gaming is different from video adventure gaming in that it can employ both physical and virtual objects to tell stories. According to Kanter(2004), interactive environments integrates physical and virtual worlds into a mixed-reality. It is suggested that the player can interact with physical objects and influence events in the virtual world from the interaction. How physical environments use surrounded objects to tell stories becomes another important issue to be discussed.

According to gaming theorist Jenkins(2004), there are four kinds of environmental storytelling. The first kind of storytelling is vocative spaces. This kind does not so much tell self-contained stories as draw upon our previously existing narrative competencies. An example is Disney's Haunted Mansion. The second kind is enacting stories. Narratives can also enter games on the level of localized events. An example is the Odessa Steps sequence in Sergei Eisenstein's *Battleship Potempkin*. The third one is the detective story which is the classic illustration of this principle. Narrative comprehension is an active process by which viewers assemble and make hypotheses from textual cues and clues. The fourth kind is emergent narratives. They are not pre-structured or pre-programmed, instead they are taking shape through the game play. Each design of plot is ripe with narrative possibilities.

However, not all environmental narratives are suitable to guide learners' discovery learning. Evocative space stories require learners to have shared prior knowledge and experiences. Hence it is difficult to apply in class with different learners. Furthermore, embedded stories only enhance learners' experiences without considering the relationship between the single plot and the whole story. Hence, it is not suitable to guide learners.

Taking all the factors above into consideration, the flow chart can be used to design the whole narrative structure, the hidden story can be designed for emergent stories and the braided plot can be designed for embedded stories. Hence, these texts are best suited for designing mobile gaming narratives in interactive environments for guided discovery learning.

5   Method

The research method I use is textual analysis to analyze "Façade" (http://www.interactivestory.net), an adventure game which focuses on environmental story design. Michael Mateas and Andrew Stern, the de-signers of Façade introduce the game as follows:

Façade is an artificial intelligence-based experiment in an electronic narra-tive – an attempt to move beyond traditional branching or hyper-linked narratives to create a fully-realized, one-act interactive drama. The player plays the character of a long time friend of Grace and Trip, an attractive and materially successful couple in their early thirties. During an evening get-together at their apartment that quickly turns ugly, the player becomes entangled in the high-conflict dissolution of Grace's and Trip's marriage.

Figure 10: The characters in Façade (Mateas, M. and Stern, A., 2005,from http://www.interactivestory.net)

Façade is a critical case since it deploys all kinds of clues in a geographical location to tell a nonlinear story and guides the player from the storylines. In research procedure design, the researcher has to play through every scenario of Façade. For example, the research has to try to react to Grace's or Trip's conversations differently. If Grace asks what you think about the painting, the researcher has to answer positively the first time and negatively the second time. The researcher has to try every possible reaction to get all possible scenarios of Façade in order to get its whole text and the different choices offered from different nodes.

In the data analysis, I will analyze Façade's narrative structure and most importantly how Façade uses all kinds of clues in the environment to guide players to play the game successfully.

6   Results and discussion

The research result shows that while the researcher reacts differently each time, there will always be three scenarios showing up. One is in the beginning, another is in the middle and the other is in the end. It suggests that there are three nodes (beginning, middle and end) which every player must go through but among each node there are various events which show up according to the player's inputs. Hence, Façade has used the flow chart design to guide the player.

Second, these different events from the nodes are not ordered in a fixed linear sequence. It means while the researcher's reaction is A in the first time, the next event could be B. However, while the researcher responds the same the second time, the next event could be C. In brief, there are different events among nodes. However, they don't always show up in the same order. Hence, every time when the player plays, he/she will have a different play experience.

Third, while events don't show up in a fixed order, each event has strong logical consistency. The user has to detect the relation between each event to decide the next step. For example, the player first has to get familiar with Grace's and Trip's personalities. Second, the player has to form the hypothesis of the possible reactions of both Grace and Trip. Third, the player has to test the hypothesis. According to the hypothesis, the player has to decide how to react to Grace's and Trip's conversation. Finally, the player has to reflect if the prediction is in line with the script. If it is not consistent, Grace and Trip will start to react strangely and contradict their previous behaviour. Hence, it is a guided discovery process in which the player has to use all the clues to find out the story by trial-and-error. Besides, the user can click any objects in the virtual space to find out the embedded stories. For example, when the player touches the painting, the couple starts to fight about the painting. Hence, it uses the clues in the surroundings to tell an embedded story.

Furthermore, the user can gradually figure out what happened from the characters' conversation. Hence, it uses the braided plot to tell an embedded and emergent story. Besides, the results are decided by the user's input. Hence, there is no "absolute" ending. Grace and Trip may forgive each other or continue to fight. The player (the guest) may be appreciated or asked to leave. Above all, Façade uses embedded narratives and emergent narratives to tell an interactive story. This story requires the user to discover the story actively by himself or herself.

In conclusion, I suggest that in designing mobile gaming narratives into interactive environments for guided discovery learning, teachers should consider which location is an important node that every learner has to go through. However, between the important node, teachers should provide different events for learners to choose, including wrong ones. The different events don't need to have a fixed order. Hence, the learner can have different play experiences every time when he/she plays. However, different events should be consistent to be able to guide learners. Finally, teachers also need to consider different possible ending scenarios according to learners' self-construction. Hence, the learner can evaluate his/her learning outcomes by himself/herself.

In application into mobile interactive environments, the teacher should set the important nodes in different physical environments which all students have to go through. For example, the teacher can set the nodes in the classroom or the gate of college buildings. Other nodes can be located in different places according to the learner's everyday life such as his/her house, bus station etc. Since there are many objects in the surroundings, teachers should also provide clues of the next location or physical objects by mobile message between different nodes. With all the work above, mobile gaming narratives for guided discovery learning in interactive environments can make learners play and learn anywhere and anytime.

7 Conclusions and suggestions

This study integrates education, narratives and gaming theories to explore the possibilities of designing gaming narratives into mobile interactive environments for guided discovery learning. The findings in this study suggest that the game genres of adventure games, interactive narratives of the flow chart, the hidden story and the braided plot can be designed to guide learners in mobile interactive environments. Furthermore, environmental designs of emergent and embedded stories can be applied in a mixed-reality to tell stories.

Via the analysis of the critical case Façade, some design suggestions for teachers are provided. However, most adventure game genres are restricted to one-person adventure game types. Hence, it is difficult to foster collaborative learning activities. Further research can be investigated about the possibilities to extend one-person adventure games into multi-persons adventure games to be able to support more collaborative learning activities.

References

Bădut(2004.06) "A perspective over the location-based applications/services – LBS/LBA", Paper read at 10th EC GI & GIS Workshop, ESDI State of the Art, Warsaw, Poland, June.

Bruner, J. S. (1961) "The act of discovery", Harvard Educational Review, Vol. 31, pp. 21-32.

Cavallari, B, Hedberg, J and Harper, B (1992) "Adventure games in education: a review",
Australian Journal of Educational Technology, Vol. 8, No. 2, pp.172-184.
http://www.ascilite.org.au/ajet/ajet8/cavallari.html

Dillon, T. (2004) "adventure Games for Learning and Storytelling," [online], future lab,
http://www.futurelab.org.uk/resources/documents/project_reports/Adventure_Author_context_paper.pdf

Dondlinger, M. J. (2007) "Educational Video Game Design: A Review of the Literature", Journal of Applied Educational Technology, Vol. 4, No.1, Spring, pp. 21-31.

Heidemann, S., and Hewitt, D., (1992) Pathways to Play: Developing Play Skills in Young Children, Redleaf Press, MN..

Jenkins, H.(2004) 'Game Design as Narrative Architecture', in Noah Wardrip-Fruin and Pat Harrigan (ed.), First Person: New Media as Story, Performance and Game(pp118-130), MIT Press ,Cambridge.

Kanter(2000) "An Application Architecture for Mobile Interactive Spaces", Paper read at 3th IEEE Workshop on Mobile Computing Systems and Applications, Monterey, CA, USA, December.

Kirschner, P. A., Sweller, J. & Clark, R. E. (2006) "Why minimal guidance during instruction does not work: an analysis of the failure of constructivist, discovery, problem-based, experiential, and inquiry-based teaching", Educational Psychologist, Vol. 41, No. 2, pp. 75-86.

Koskinen, Veitonen, Laaksonen and Väänänen (2005) 'New Generation Wireless Technologies impact on Educational Environments Case: Utilizing Finnish Sign Language in Interpreter Training', Conference Proceedings, the International Workshop on Wireless and Mobile Technologies in Education, Tokushima, Japan, pp. 200-202.

Mayer, R. (2004) "Should there be a three-strikes rule against pure discovery learning? The case for guided methods of instruction", American Psychologist, Vol. 59, No.1, Winter, pp.14-19.

New South Wales Department of Education (1989). Mathematics K-6 (current syllabus), Sydney: NSW Department of Education.

Rollings, A. and Adams, E. (2003) Andrew Rollings and Ernest Adams on game design, New Riders Publishing, USA.

Ryan, M-L (2001) Narrative as virtual reality : immersion and interactivity in literature and electronic media, Johns Hopkins University Press, Baltimore, Md.

Smilansky, S. & Shefatya, L. (1990) Facilitating play: A medium for promoting cognitive, socio-emotional and academic achievement in young children, Psycho educational and Educational Pubs, Gaithersburg , Maryland.

Thomas, J. M., and Young, R. M.,(2007) 'Becoming Scientists: Employing Adaptive Interactive Narrative to Guide Discovery Learning', Conference Proceedings, the AIED-07 Workshop on Narrative Learning Environments, Marina Del Rey, California, USA.

Ling-yi Huang

Veermans, K. (2002). Intelligent support for discovery learning. Using opportunistic learner modelling and heuristics to support simulation based discovery learning. Unpublished doctoral dissertation, Twente University, Enschede.